ROYAL AIR FORCE RESERVE AND AUXILIARY FORCES

ROYAL AIR FORCE HISTORICAL SOCIETY

2

Copyright 2003: Royal Air Force Historical Society

First published in the UK in 2003 by the Royal Air Force Historical Society

ISBN 0-9530345-1-8

Typeset by Creative
115 Magdalen Road
Oxford
OX4 1RS

Printed by Advance Book Printing
Unit 9 Northmoor Park
Church Road
Northmoor
OX29 5UH

CONTENTS

SUPPLEMENTARY PAPERS

4

ROYAL AIR FORCE RESERVE CLASSES

In order to keep up with changing circumstances, the regulations governing reserve personnel have been subject to progressive refinement over time. Thus, for instance, when it became necessary to distinguish between ex-regular (Class A) pilots and direct entrant reservists the latter were categorised as Class AA which then had to be subdivided into Classes AA1 and AA2 to differentiate between those who already knew how to fly and those who would need to be taught. Similarly, the training commitments evolved through time, those noted below generally being those applicable when each Class was first introduced.

Auxiliary, Special Reserve, Volunteer Reserve and Reserve forces all had their own sets of regulations, but these arrangements were not exclusive. In the 1930s, for instance, it was possible for an ex-regular Class C reservist to be holding a current commission in the AAF.

Class	Remarks
A	Conceived 1918; implemented 1923. Ex-regular commissioned pilots (12 hrs/yr).
AA1	Direct entrant officers with some previous flying experience, eg ex-UAS (12 hrs/yr).
AA2	Direct entrant officers with no previous flying experience (12 hrs/yr).
B	Conceived 1918; implemented 1923. Ex-regular technical officers requiring up-to-date knowledge (14 days/yr if required).
BB	Technical officers with no previous regular service experience requiring up-to-date knowledge (14 days/yr if required).
C	Conceived 1918; implemented 1923. Ex-regular/wartime technical and other officers, eg accountants, not requiring up-to-date knowledge (no mandatory training but up to 14 days/yr permitted).
CC	Non-specialist civilians in RAF employ who would be commissioned on mobilisation (no training).
D	Conceived 1918; implemented 1923. Ex-regular doctors & dentists (no training during mandatory reserve period but up to 14 days/yr if extended).

DD   Doctors & dentists with no previous regular service experience (no mandatory training).

E   Conceived 1918; implemented 1923. Ex-regular airmen (up to 14 days/yr if required but 12 hrs/yr mandatory for airmen pilots).

F   Established circa 1935. Airmen pilots with no previous regular service experience (30 hrs/yr). Entry into Class F (the NCO equivalent of Class AA2) ceased following establishment of RAFVR in 1937.

G   Established 1945. Released ex-regular and reserve airmen engaged to serve 'for the present emergency' (the Army equivalent was Class Z). No routine training commitment but liable for recall while in reserve. Last intake 31 December 48; liability to recall terminated 30 June 59.

H   Established 1 January 49 for ex-airmen subject to the 1948 National Service Act. Originally 6, later $3^{1}/_{2}$, year's reserve training liability (not more than 21 days in any one year up to a total of 60); this obligation terminated 30 June 64.

J   Established circa 1948. Similar to Class CC in that it comprised civilians who might be required to exercise executive authority and/or wear uniform on mobilisation, but only in a specific locality, ie they could not be posted (without their consent).

NOTE: The regulations relating to reserve service in general, and to obligations in particular, over a period of roughly half-a-century are far too complex to summarise comprehensively here. While essentially accurate, therefore, the above can be regarded only as an *aide memoir* and it should not be quoted as a definitive reference.

SELECTED ABBREVIATIONS

A&SD	Administrative and Special Duties (Branch)
AAF	Auxiliary Air Force
AASF	Advanced Air Striking Force
ACAS	Assistant Chief of the Air Staff
ADCC	Air Defence Cadet Corps
AFRes	(US) Air Force Reserve
AFU	Advanced Flying Unit
AID	Aeronautical Inspection Directorate
ALBE	Air League of the British Empire
AMP	Air Member for Personnel
ANG	(US) Air National Guard
ATC	Air Training Corps
BALPA	British Air Line Pilots Association
CCF	Combined Cadet Force
DGT	Director General of Training
EOD	Explosive Ordnance Disposal
ERFTS	Elementary and Reserve Flying Training School
FCU	Fighter Control Unit
FRG	Federal Republic of Germany
GCA	Ground Controlled Approach
IOT	Initial Officer Training
JMC	Joint Maritime Course
JMOTS	Joint Maritime Operations Training Staff
KIA	Killed in Action
LAA	Light Anti-Aircraft
LAW	Light Anti-tank Weapon
MAMS	Mobile Air Movements Squadron
MC	(NATO) Military Committee (as in MC 14/3)
MHQ	Maritime Headquarters
MHU	Maritime Headquarters Unit
NLA	National League of Airmen
NSA	National Service Act
PFB	Preliminary Flying Badge
PRO	Public Record Office
RAuxAF	Royal Auxiliary Air Force
RAFO	Reserve of Air Force Officers
RAFRO	Royal Air Force Reserve of Officers

RAFSC	RAF Support Command
RAFVR	Royal Air Force Volunteer Reserve
RFS	Reserve Flying School
RMP	Recognised Maritime Picture
SAR	Search And Rescue
SERE	Special Entrant and Re-Entrant (Course)
SHORAD	SHOrt Range Air Defence
SOP	Standard Operational Procedure(s)
STC	Strike Command TAF Tactical Air Force
TAFA	Territorial and Auxiliary Forces Association
TAVRA	Territorial, Auxiliary and Volunteer Reserve Association
TTW	Transition To War
UAS	University Air Squadron
VFR	Visual Flight Rules
VR	Volunteer Reserve

Halcyon days. A Wapiti of No 605 Sqn

RAF RESERVE FORCES
RAF MUSEUM, HENDON, 23rd OCTOBER 2002
WELCOME ADDRESS BY THE SOCIETY'S CHAIRMAN
Air Vice-Marshal Nigel Baldwin CB CBE FRAeS

Ladies and Gentlemen. Welcome to the Society's autumn seminar at which we are going to address a very important subject; a distinct, but perhaps unsung, aspect of the Royal Air Force's history. It is a fact, one that we often tend to lose sight of, that most of the fighting in WW II was done by 'reservists' of one kind or another, so today we are going to trace the contribution made by various reserve and auxiliary air forces from 1912 onwards.

Before I introduce our Chairman for the day, let me express my usual thanks to Dr Michael Fopp and his staff here at the Museum, for allowing us to use their excellent facilities and for helping us so much with the production of the day. I must also thank Tony Freeman, who provided the inspiration for this project, and Jeff Jefford, who has done a great deal behind the scenes to ensure that we have a full and comprehensive programme.

There is a great deal of experience in the room and I take particular pleasure in welcoming a galaxy of former Inspector Generals. Lord Monro, known to many of you as Sir Hector Monro, is a former Honorary Inspector General as is Air Chf Mshl Sir John Barraclough. I also welcome Gp Capts Robins and Harris, both of whom are former Inspectors of the Royal Auxiliary Air Force. To oversee the day's events, I am grateful to the present, and youngest, Honorary Inspector General, AVM Barry Newton. An instructor of mine when I was a flight cadet at Cranwell, Barry has spent much of the last few years on reserve business and has just the experience we need to guide us through the day.

Barry, you have control.

INTRODUCTION BY SEMINAR CHAIRMAN
Air Vice-Marshal Barry Newton CB OBE

My Lord, Ladies and Gentlemen. Thank you, Nigel, for that introduction. With my father and my grandfather in the audience, I am obviously going to have to watch my Ps and Q's today! I was reminded when I was thinking about this seminar of the man who staggered out of Sothebys carrying a enormous grandfather clock which knocked an old lady into the gutter. 'You stupid man!' she said, 'Why can't you wear a wristwatch like everyone else?!' Now getting things into the right perspective is very much what the Royal Air Force Historical Society is all about and it is a great privilege for me to be invited to chair today's seminar.

In 1930, when Lord Trenchard left the Air Ministry, he said, 'I have laid the foundations for a castle. If no one builds more than a cottage on them, it will at least be a jolly good cottage.' As we shall hear today, Reserve Forces were very much part of those foundations and particularly close to Trenchard's heart. We will examine the genesis and evolution of, specifically, the Auxiliary Air Force, because it did not become 'Royal' until 1947, the Special Reserve and the Royal Air Force Volunteer Reserve and consider how effectively they have been employed. I apologise in advance on behalf of the team that we were unable to find the time to talk about the Women's Auxiliary Air Force. We hope to do that on a future occasion.

This morning's programme will take us from 1912 to 1945, apart from the UASs which we will cover after lunch, and then go on to consider the contributions of the post-war Royal Auxiliary Air Force and RAFVR, before hearing from former and current auxiliary officers about the Royal Auxiliary Air Force Regiment and the roles of the Movements and Aeromedical Evacuation Squadrons.

We will round off both the morning and afternoon sessions with discussion periods and, in order to avoid becoming involved in current issues, the cut-off point for these will be the Gulf War.

AIR FORCE RESERVES 1912 TO MUNICH

Wing Commander 'Jeff' Jefford

'Jeff' joined the RAF in 1959 as a pilot but (was) soon remustered as a navigator. His flying experience included tours with Nos 45, 83 and 50 Sqns and instructing at No 6 FTS. Administrative and staff appointments involved sundry jobs at Manby, Gatow, Brampton and a total of eight years at HQ Strike Command. He took early retirement in 1991 to read history at London University. He has three books to his credit and has been a member of the Society's Executive Committee since 1998; he is currently editor of its Journal.

The concept of men having an obligation to contribute to communal defence must surely be as old as society itself. It was certainly fundamental to the feudal system and we have, for instance, Falstaff's 15th Century, Wars-of-the-Roses-style recruiting exercise in Henry IV, Pt 2. Or perhaps that was medieval conscription? Whichever it was, three-and-a-half centuries later the Militia Act of 1757 created county-based forces which could be raised in an emergency. In 1794 provision was made for the raising of volunteer regiments to counter the threat of invasion by Napoleon; in 1867 the Army Reserve Act provided for a trained reserve of 80 000 men, and so on. The point that I am trying to make is that there was nothing new in the idea of auxiliary and reserve forces when military aviation came along in 1912. The organisation in vogue at that time had been reformed as recently as 1907 when Haldane had replaced the militia and the volunteers with a system of territorial regiments raised by County Associations – the TA.

The ground rules on which the Royal Flying Corps was to be established were laid down in a Royal Warrant which was promulgated in a Special Army Order of 15 April 1912. In effect the RFC's Birth Certificate, this document provided for officers from other branches of the army (or from the navy) to be seconded to the Corps for four year's continuous service after which they were to return to their regiments, although there was a possibility of extensions of service, a year at a time. Alternatively, after learning how to fly, regular officers could immediately resume their regimental duties but now annotated as members of the RFC Reserve, which meant that they were liable to recall for flying duties at any time over the next four years. Finally, as with other branches of the Service, the RFC had taken advantage of another of Haldane's 1907 innovations by establishing its own Branch of the Special Reserve. Special Reservists were men who had not previously served as regulars and this arrangement permitted civilians to learn to fly at the War Office's expense and then to hold a reserve commission, initially for four years although this too could be extended a year at a time. Under certain circumstances it was possible for Special Reservists to serve full time but most did not. The implications of all this are not perhaps immediately apparent but the fact is that the pre-war RFC had no *regular* officers that it could call its own. Most pilots were serving on secondment; the few who were directly recruited were Special Reservists.[1]

All of this became somewhat academic in August 1914 when war was declared and reservists were called up. When the first element of the RFC crossed the Channel it included 105 officers of whom eleven were Special Reservists.[2] There were not a lot of changes over the next three years, most wartime RFC officers being either transferees from the trenches already holding (or about to be granted) temporary 'for the duration only' commissions on the General List or directly enlisted personnel who were commissioned into the RFC Special Reserve, which now automatically meant active service.

The next significant event occurred in November 1917 when the Air Force (Constitution) Act was passed. This document represents the RAF's Birth Certificate and Section 6 says:

'It shall be lawful for His Majesty to raise and maintain an Air Force Reserve and an Auxiliary Air Force......'

---

[1]Conditions were different for non-commissioned personnel. While warrant officers and men of the regular army could also transfer to the Corps for a four-year stint, the RFC could directly recruit soldiers for four year's active service plus four in the reserve.
[2]Provision was made for NCOs and ORs within the Special Reserve from 1912 but there do not appear to have been any enlistments until 1914, the RFC having twenty-five Special Reservist soldiers on its books when war was declared. All were called up between 5 and 15 August; all remained in the UK initially, mostly with Nos 1 and 6 Sqns, but the majority were in France by April 1915.

No one was going to do very much about that in the middle of a major war, of course, but it clearly shows that those concerned with such matters had thought about it. Once the war was over, consideration began to be given to the provision of reserves and there was some mention of this within the famous Trenchard Memorandum of late 1919. Section 4 envisaged that sufficient ex-wartime personnel could be relied upon to respond to any minor crises that might crop up in the short term. For the future it offered no concrete proposals but suggested the possibility of reservists being trained on an individual basis and/or within dedicated units, some of which, it was thought, might be sponsored by industry. This might have been a proto-'Public Private Finance Initiative', but, in the event, the idea came to naught.

In practice, of course, the potential for creating a reserve had existed long before Trenchard put pen to paper because, as they were paid off, the officers and airmen being demobilised in droves from early 1919 onwards had all been registered under legislation borrowed from the Army. At this stage it was anticipated that there would be only Classes A to E, although these would later be progressively subdivided and others would be added. Work to refine and formalise the constitution of a specifically *air force* reserve and to create its supporting legal framework had begun in late 1918. This project progressed only slowly, however, and it was December 1921 before the King was able to initial the final version of the enabling Royal Warrant.[3]

Post-war uncertainty, budgetary constraint and inter-Service rivalry prevented much more progress being made until 1923 when the Salisbury Committee finally clarified the relationships between the RAF, the RN and the Army and, based on the need to counter the French, who were characterised as 'The Continental Menace', laid down a blueprint for a 'Home Defence Force' of 52 squadrons.

The Air Ministry promptly set up a Mobilisation Committee to consider the implications of operating and sustaining a metropolitan air force of that size in wartime (plus an Expeditionary Force of eight squadrons and the FAA). Remarkably, this committee would eventually conclude that this would require a personnel reserve of some 6500 officers and 19 000 airmen to fly and maintain more than 8000 aeroplanes and 14 000 engines.

[3]King's Order 105 of 21 Dec 21.

Plainly this was quite out of the question but, until the 52-squadron force actually existed, it was also a question that did not need to be answered – and even the most optimistic of projections did not see the 52-squadron scheme being fully implemented in less than five years. In the event the plan was revised annually and its completion was progressively postponed, or 'decelerated' as it was termed, so that by 1930 it was not expected to be complete until as late as 1938, by which time it would have long since been overtaken by events.

Since the mega-air force was not expected to materialise for several years, the Service was amply provided for in the short term by the Air Estimates for 1923-24 which had sanctioned a more realistic reserve establishment of 700 pilots and 12 000 airmen.[4] The bulk of the pilots were to be officers completing engagements on Short Service Commissions. The short service scheme, originally entailing three years' regular plus four years' reserve service[5], had been introduced in July 1919 so the first cohort was just beginning to emerge in 1923 and it was expected that about 100 would be available to join the recently established Reserve of Air Force Officers[6] – the RAFO – by April of that year, with a steady stream joining them thereafter. Clearly, it would be several years before the total of 700 would be reached so, in the meantime, it was hoped to make up the numbers required by persuading wartime veterans and commercial pilots to enlist voluntarily as reservists.

The reserve having become a tangible presence in 1923, it was axiomatic that provision would have to be made for periodic refresher

---

[4]Some sources maintain that there had been an establishment of 200 reserve pilots prior to this. Precise details appear to be lacking, but, since there were no legislative, organisational or administrative arrangements in place to support such a reserve, and no provision appears to have been made for refresher flying, if it existed at all, it must have been a very low key affair.

[5]To begin with, an additional year of regular service was an optional extra, although four years had become the standard engagement before the end of 1920. The options of one, two and three year extensions were introduced in 1922 but the basic engagement was up to five years by 1928 and in 1932-33 it was as long as six years. The four years in the RAFO was merely the contractual obligation; if mutually acceptable, one could undertake to extend this period voluntarily.

[6]Although the creation of the RAFO, and the necessary draft regulations, had been given royal approval in December 1921 (see Note 3), it was not given substance until February 1923, when it first began to feature in the Air Force List, the necessary 'rule book', in the form of the first edition of AP 938, being published in March.

OPERATOR	WHERE	WHEN
De Havilland	Stag Lane	1 May 23
Bristol	Filton	28 May 23
Beardmore	Renfrew	24 Jul 23
Armstrong Whitworth	Whitley	31 Jul 23
North Sea Aerial and General Transport (Blackburn)	Brough	21 May 24

Fig 1. The five commercial schools engaged to provide refresher training on Air Ministry contracts.

training. Some consideration was given to expanding the Service flying training organisation but it was eventually concluded that it would be preferable to contract civilian firms to provide flying facilities at a rate of about 12 hours per year per pilot.

The upshot of this was the establishment of the five Reserve Flying Schools shown at Figure 1. In 1923 the cost of this scheme was expected to be about £125 000 per annum plus a similar sum to cover the pay of reserve airmen and it was anticipated that the total would rise to £375 000 when the reserve was at full strength. That would have represented about 2.5% of the Air Estimates of the period or, if you prefer, about £13M in today's money. In the event the sums had been way off the mark and a year's experience showed that the schools needed to be paid almost twice as much per flying hour to remain viable and, even then Beardmores were unable to make ends meet and they declined to renew their contract when it came up for review in 1928.

There had been some problems in building the reserve up to its authorised strength and in the spring of 1926 it was still about 200 pilots short of the 700 required.[7] To supplement the numbers, therefore, it had been decided to introduce direct recruiting into the RAFO. That implied a need for *ab initio* flying training and an intake of fifty per year was authorised (sixty from 1929). Each man was allocated 30 hours at a Reserve Flying School.

---

[7]The Air Force List for March 1926 identifies 489 RAFO pilots, thirty-two of them being direct entrants. There may also have been a small, but undetermined, number of airmen pilots registered within Class E.

16

One of the old Blackburn Kangaroos used at Brough to provide multi-engined refresher training for reservists in the mid-1920s.

Most of the aeroplanes used for refresher flying by the civilian schools were adaptations of wartime designs. The school at Filton, for instance, used variations on the Bristol Fighter theme. Blackburns offered something a little more exotic at Brough where multi-engine flying was available on old war-surplus Kangaroos and where one could renew one's seaplane ticket on a Dart.

By the early 1930s most of these old war horses were overdue for replacement and the Ministry decided, as a matter of policy, to dispense with the relatively large and heavy, quasi 'Service' types in favour of light elementary trainers. From 1933 the civilian schools began to standardise on the Tiger Moth and the Blackburn B.2. Because these aeroplanes were so much cheaper to operate, the allocation of refresher hours could be raised to 20 per year and the *ab initio* syllabus to 50.

The next major change occurred in 1935 when, partially in response to the demands of the Expansion Schemes, the Air Ministry introduced an entirely new flying training sequence. The first phase was now going to be provided at civilian-manned schools which would acquire quasi-military status in December 1937 when they were designated as numbered Elementary and Reserve Flying Training Schools (ERFTS).

The first four prospective ERFTSs were created from the four remaining Reserve Flying Schools and they provided the model for the immediate formation of a further nine; there were more than forty by the

CLASS	Nos		AVAILABILITY	Nos
A	544		Straight to a squadron	137
AA	249		Need 6 weeks at FTS	132
C	227		Need 12 weeks at FTS	418
E	77		Need 16 weeks at FTS	600
F	351		Not available	161
TOTAL	**1448**		**TOTAL**	**1448**

*Fig 2. Numbers and availability of pilots within the
Reserve as at 1 April 1935.*

time that war was declared. Thereafter, apart from Cranwell cadets, the ERFTSs conducted *all* RAF elementary flying instruction while continuing to provide refresher facilities for reserve pilots.

There were now almost 1500 reservists, partly because of the increasing outflow of short-service pilots from an expanding air force, and partly because the annual intake of direct entrant reservists had been raised to (up to) 300, all of whom were trained alongside regulars on the same 56-day, 50-hour ERFTS course.

Having said that there were about 1500 reserve pilots by 1935, it is worth looking at the constitution of this group. Figure 2 shows the breakdown of the headcount as at 1 April. What these people represented was the first wave of replacements for pilots lost in action. Unfortunately, 41% of the total were direct entrant reservists (Classes AA and F) who had completed only the 50-hour elementary course (which stopped short of the award of a flying badge), so they would clearly need to be given a lot more training before they could be even remotely regarded as being fit to fly on operations. Furthermore, pilots registered as Class C were supposedly enlisted for ground, not flying, duties.

Figure 2 also shows the overall availability of these pilots. As you can see, only 9% of them could be regarded as being immediately available for operations and, because they were in protected occupations, 11% were not available at all. Depending upon their basic level of competence and/or the time that had elapsed since they last wore uniform, the other 80% required between six weeks and four months of additional training.

While this might seem to be a trifle unrealistic, we should perhaps remember that the pace of life was rather slower than it is today and this sort of readiness had sufficed during an era in which defence policy had been predicated upon there being no major war for ten years. The revelation of the existence of the *Luftwaffe* in 1935 invalidated that posture and meant that the provision of reserves was no longer adequate. A new approach was clearly needed but I will leave later pre-war innovations to one of my colleagues.

So much for the provision of reserve pilots. I suspect that some of you might expect me to say something about observers. The RAF had more or less decided to do without commissioned back-seaters almost as soon as the shooting had stopped back in 1918. We need not debate the whys and wherefores of that decision but there were clearly a few officers who had reservations over its wisdom.

In 1923 the first edition of AP938, the regulations governing reserve service, was published and, perhaps as a result of the thinking exercises that its drafting had involved, questions had been raised over the need for reserve observer officers. AMP, Oliver Swann, recommended that 100 ex-wartime observers should be recruited into the reserve and, a little surprisingly, Trenchard actually agreed. They were to be assigned to Class B, however, which categorised them, not as aviators, but as technical officers with an annual refresher training commitment, although CAS had made it crystal clear that the air force could not actually afford to provide observers with any training at all! No change there then, and, it is hardly surprising that nothing like the required 100 ex-observer officers were prepared to sign up for a second dose of ritual humiliation. The RAFO Section of the Air Force List for March 1926, for instance, includes about forty.[8]

As regards airmen, like officers, their regular engagements included a commitment to spend a post-completion period in the reserve, including, for some trades, a liability to recall for continuation training, although this seems to have been little exercised.

Thus far I have dealt only with the personnel of, what we might regard as, the 'ordinary' RAF Reserve up to the mid-1930s. We now need to address the cases of the Auxiliary Air Force and the Special Reserve, each of which was constituted quite separately, so I now need to backtrack ten

[8]There are, in the March 1926 List, forty-four Class B officers who had been graded as observers during WW I; it is quite possible, however, that some of them may have registered for reserve service in technical disciplines, rather than as observers.

or fifteen years. While Trenchard's 1919 Memorandum had made some mention of auxiliaries, it was 1922 before firm proposals began to emerge, the Air Estimates for 1923-24 eventually announcing, as an initial contribution towards the projected 52-squadron scheme, the formation (over the next few years) of an additional fifteen regular squadrons plus five auxiliary squadrons.

This represented something of a change of heart as some influential figures (including Mr Churchill) had previously been of the opinion that it would be impossible for non-regulars to attain the levels of skill and efficiency that would be required. On the other hand, the price tag attached to the 52-squadron scheme was somewhat daunting and the partial substitution of part-time units and personnel was, quite plainly, a way of reducing the expense. It should be clearly understood, however, that, while they might have had 'auxiliary' status in terms of availability and readiness, these squadrons were not 'extras'; they were to constitute an integral element of the 52-squadron plan.

While the Air Force (Constitution) Act of 1917 had made provision for regulations relating to the Territorial Army to be applied to the projected air auxiliaries, this rather *ad hoc* arrangement was hardly satisfactory so the first thing that needed to be done was to provide the air force with something a little more specific. The result was the Auxiliary Air Force and Air Force Reserve Bill which was laid before the House in March 1924.

Once that had been enacted it remained to approach the Council of County Territorial Associations to arrange for them to assume their new responsibilities. The organisations in those counties which were directly involved subsequently became Territorial Army *and* Air Force Associations. Their responsibilities were very extensive, covering recruiting, pay, clothing (for airmen), liaison with civilian employers, the provision of land, accommodation and equipment, including rifle ranges, armouries, MT – and horses! The necessary funding was embedded within the annual Air Estimates but there was clearly a great deal of administrative work involved, including an annual budgeting exercise.

All of this was a bit complicated, but so was the RAF's approach, mainly because it was breaking new ground and having to feel its way. It decided to adopt two styles of organisation to see which was more successful in attracting recruits. Figure 3 highlights the main differences between the concepts of an Auxiliary and of a Special Reserve Squadron.

First of all, they were to be designated separately and additionally to, rather than within, the established sequence of regular squadron number plates. As you can also see, in effect, the auxiliaries were to have 'amateur' status, practically all of their manpower, being recruited, and largely trained, locally. Note that, despite what it says about an AAF officer's having to be a licensed pilot, that implied no more than an ability to fly an Avro 504 or a Moth and there was a lot more to it if you were going to fly a bomber – even so, the regulations required an AAF pilot to fly only the same 12 hours per year as a fully trained ex-regular in the RAFO. This 12 hours (raised to 25 during the 1930s), which was supposed to be spread evenly across the year, was only a minimum, of course, and it specifically excluded the flying undertaken during the annual camp.

The Special Reserve units were far more robust in that they had a substantial core of regulars and their volunteer airmen were to be recruited as qualified tradesmen requiring little more than Service indoctrination. Another way of looking at the Special Reserves would be to regard them as cadre squadrons and, with the passage of time, they were increasingly referred to as such.

When these ideas were crystallising in 1924 the plan had called for there to be an eventual total of thirteen squadrons, seven within the special reserve and six auxiliary; all were to operate in the bomber role. By the time that the thirteenth unit had actually materialised it would be 1931 and the breakdown actually turned out to be eight auxiliaries and only five cadres.

So far as higher levels of organisation were concerned, the man in charge at the beginning was the Superintendent of the Reserve, Wg Cdr Frank Haskins, but in 1925, when the first squadrons began to form, an operational formation, HQ Special Reserve and Auxiliary Air Force, was set up in Sloane Square. The first AOC was Air Cdre Cyril Newall who was succeeded by Air Cdre John Hearson at the end of the year, by which time one SR and four AAF squadrons had been formed, albeit, as yet, on little more than a nucleus basis; a brace of Avros and a couple of 'Ninaks' each in the case of the auxiliaries, rather more aeroplanes for the semi-regular cadres.

	AUXILIARY	SPECIAL RESERVE
Designation	600-series	500-series
Recruiting	Via the County Association	Directly by the unit
Qualification of officers	Licensed pilot	Taught to fly by unit
Qualification of airmen	Trade training provided by unit	Pre-skilled
Organisation	Three flights of AAF personnel with small HQ staff of regulars	HQ and one flight of regulars plus one (or two) SR flight(s)
CO	AAF officer	Regular RAF officer
Siting	Near centres of population	Near engineering centres
Training	Frequent attendance at Town HQ and local airfield plus annual camp	Limited attendance by SR for Service familiarisation and discipline

Fig 3. Broad comparison of the characteristics of an Auxiliary, as compared to a Special Reserve, Squadron when the system was first conceived.

This arrangement did not last for long, however, and in 1927 the controlling formation became No 1 (Air Defence) Group. By that time Air Cdre Hearson had already decided that the 600-series auxiliary units were the way to go and he proposed that the 500-series cadres should be converted to auxiliary status. The Air Council thought it a bit previous to be drawing such conclusions after little more than a year's experience, and the proposal was put on ice.

It surfaced again in 1930, this time sponsored by the Establishments Committee. The relevant facts were that one of the key distinctions between the SR and AAF units, whether or not their pilots were qualified on enlistment, had become blurred, because the SR was now accepting trained pilots while the AAF had started to provide in-house *ab initio* flying training. More importantly, however, recruiting of *airmen* for the Special Reserve had proved to be less straightforward than had been anticipated, because men had been reluctant to enlist in trades for which they were already qualified.

On reflection, it was perhaps understandable that a skilled metal-worker, for instance, might well feel that he had had more than enough exposure to tin-bashing during the week and if he was going to sign on to work at weekends he wanted to do it as a 'chippy' or an electrician. This was not what the air force had had in mind, of course, but in order to get anywhere near the recruiting targets, many SR airmen had been accepted on these terms and to provide the necessary cross-training COs had been obliged to mix their reservists with their regular personnel throughout the squadron. As a result, neither flight was exclusively manned by regulars, which more or less nullified the cadre concept. In effect, the SR units were tending to function as AAF squadrons but with a much higher proportion of, expensive, full-time personnel – which was, no doubt, what had attracted the attention of the establishers.

The arguments put forward in favour of the AAF are outlined at Figure 4. As you can see, they appeared to be a better prospect on almost all counts. They were certainly cheaper, possibly better, and their undoubted *esprit de corps,* arising from the degree of local support that they attracted as a result of their being almost 100% locally recruited, was likely to be invaluable in an emergency.

By comparison, the SR cadres had proved to be relatively expensive and unattractive. It took a surprisingly long time for action to be taken on this but in 1936 Air Cdre John Quinnell's No 1 (Air Defence) Group was

CRITERION	AAF v SR
Economy	Far fewer (expensive) regulars in AAF.
Recruiting	Easier in AAF – fewer constraints.
Professional Standards	Possibly higher in AAF units.
Morale	Higher in AAF because unit 'belongs' to its members.
Mobilisation	Local people expected to flock to 'their' AAF unit in an emergency, as to the TA in 1914.
Popularity	Several County Associations had offered to sponsor additional AAF (ie not SR) units.

Fig 4. Comparison of Auxiliary versus Special Reserve concepts after five years of experience.

redesignated as No 6 (Auxiliary) Group and shortly afterwards it absorbed the five SR units, Nos 500-504 Sqns, all of which were being converted to auxiliary status, although they retained their original number plates. At much the same time, 6 Gp was subordinated to the newly formed Bomber Command.

By this time (1936), in sympathy with the expansion of the regular Service, the thirteen reserve squadrons envisaged in 1924 had become seventeen and there would be twenty by the time that war was declared. Equipment had more or less kept pace with the types being flown by the regular air force, the squadrons being progressively re-equipped with such types as Hyderabads, Horsleys, Waptis, Virginias and Harts. All of these types had been bombers, reflecting the planned role for all reserve units, but in the later 1930s this policy changed and selected squadrons began to be progressively re-equipped (or new ones formed) for air defence, army co-operation or maritime reconnaissance duties. As and when a squadron was considered to have attained a reasonable degree of operational efficiency in its role it was transferred out of Bomber Command's 6 Gp to the control of a more appropriate Group HQ.

One of the factors determining operational efficiency, of course, was manning and this was causing some concern by January 1938 when the AAF was manned to only 77% of its airmen establishment and a mere 51% with respect to officers, in effect, pilots. By this time some trends could be identified and it seems that, although it was very conveniently based at Filton, the prospect of joining No 501 Sqn appears to have had surprisingly little appeal for the workforce of the collocated Bristol Aeroplane Company and, despite the presence of engineering firms like Rustons, and Clayton and Shuttleworth, Lincoln had simply lacked the population necessary to sustain No 503 Sqn at Waddington. In fact No 503 Sqn eventually had to admit defeat and it was disbanded, its place being taken by a new No 616 Sqn at Doncaster, a location which made it reasonably accessible to Sheffield folk as well.

With the diversification of roles, it was clear that future manpower requirements would have to be more closely tailored to specific tasks and new establishments had been published by mid-1938. Fighter squadrons continued to be entitled to the 164 trained airmen that had been the notional target for all AAF units in the past, but the dwindling number of bomber squadrons were now supposed to have 213 each while the forthcoming army co-operation and maritime units were to have 198 and 228 respectively. Increasing the establishments presented a very real recruiting challenge, of course, and the overall airman manning situation on the outbreak of war, when admission to the AAF ceased abruptly, stood at only 66%, as reflected at Figure 5.[9]

There was one other major pre-war development which was of particular significance to the AAF of which I must make some mention, if only because it often tends to be overlooked. By late 1936 the Air Council had decided to establish a balloon barrage to protect London. It was to consist of ten squadrons, each having forty-five balloons and, because of their relatively static locations, it was intended that some 90% of the manpower required would be locally-recruited auxiliary personnel.

The initial arrangements were overseen by HQ 6 Gp but in March 1937 the torch was passed to a new No 30 Gp which was established within Fighter Command, Air Cdre John Hearson being recalled from retirement to become its first AOC.

---

[9]Note that the tabulated percentages as at September 1939 are calculated against the establishments published in mid-1938; it is possible that the latter may have been revised before the outbreak of war but if they had been they would have been increased, rather than reduced, so Figure 5 represents a best case. Note also that some units had not been in existence for very long, No 613 Sqn, for instance, having formed as late as March 1939, so it is hardly surprising that its manning fell somewhat short of the target.

UNIT	ROLE	EST'MENT	STRENGTH	MANNING
500 Sqn	GR	228	186	82%
501 Sqn	F	164	71	43%
502 Sqn	GR	228	162	71%
504 Sqn	F	164	101	62%
600 Sqn	F	164	126	77%
601 Sqn	F	164	122	74%
602 Sqn	F	164	107	65%
603 Sqn	F	164	124	76%
604 Sqn	F	164	130	79%
605 Sqn	F	164	99	60%
607 Sqn	F	164	122	74%
608 Sqn	GR	228	175	77%
609 Sqn	F	164	93	57%
610 Sqn	F	164	106	65%
611 Sqn	F	164	99	60%
612 Sqn	GR	228	161	71%
613 Sqn	AC	198	43	22%
614 Sqn	AC	198	112	57%
615 Sqn	F	164	108	66%
616 Sqn	F	164	114	70%
	Total	**3604**	**2361**	**66%**

Fig 5. AAF Airmen on strength in September 1939.

Recruiting began in the spring of 1938 and before the year was out it had been decided to provide similar barrages for a number of large provincial cities. There were now to be four Group HQs controlling a total of forty-seven squadrons operating 1450 balloons. Recruiting for the provincial units began early in 1939, the total manpower bill now amounting to more than 18 000 auxiliaries plus a couple of thousand regulars. To ease the problem of obtaining the huge numbers required the upper age limit for recruits was set at 50.

*A Demon of No 604 Sqn, one of the four AAF fighter squadrons called
out in response to the Munich crisis.*

Meanwhile, elements of the AAF had been put under real strain for the
first time. On 26 September 1938 four fighter squadrons (Nos 600, 601,
604 and 607 Sqns, plus Nos 906 and 907 Balloon Sqns), all by now
operating Demons, were embodied in response to the Munich crisis. I
hesitate to become embroiled in semantics but this 'embodiment'
amounted only to a call out of personnel; it specifically did *not* constitute
'mobilisation' but it was certainly enough to test the system and, so far as
it went, it worked. All four squadrons were stood down again in
November and at much the same time, and regardless of their states of
readiness, the remaining squadrons assigned to 6 Gp began to be
transferred to their respective operational commands, the last of them in
January 1939.

Since AAF squadrons were now distributed among a variety of
Groups, it was considered necessary to re-establish some form of co-
ordination and to this end a Director of the Auxiliary Air Force had been
appointed in December 1938. He was Sqn Ldr, (now acting Air Cdre)
Harald Peake, the original OC 609 Sqn. He was to advise the Air Ministry
on matters peculiar to the AAF and liase on its behalf with Commands,
Groups, the County Associations and so on. The Director did not,
however, have any executive powers.

That was the last organisational milestone until the following
September, but I will leave Chris Shores to deal with the AAF's fortunes
in war.

THE ROYAL AIR FORCE VOLUNTEER RESERVE 1936-1939

Dr Tony Mansell

Having retired from a full-time lecturing post at King's College, London a few years ago, Tony Mansell is still a Senior Visiting Research Fellow there. His research into certain élite groups within British society led him to investigate RAF pilots, with particular reference to those who flew in the Battle of Britain. He has published several articles on RAF history and also enjoys reviewing books for the Society's Journal.

Let us begin with a metaphor. We can think of the pre-war RAFVR as a piece of blue litmus paper dipped into the society of 1930s Britain and changing colour to reflect popular feelings. The Air Ministry and especially AMP's Department, knew that the colour change would be from blue to pale pink, reflecting not so much party-political allegiances but rather the growth of expectations among young people. The RAFVR was planned by men who understood the social climate of their time and its implications for the new reserve they had in mind. They designed accordingly and the RAFVR stands as a tribute to their wisdom and foresight.

The Social Scene.

Britain in the 1930s is often portrayed as a desolate place, coping with the after effects of economic depression, mass unemployment and disillusion. But things were not like that everywhere in the country. In the Home Counties, even in some of the northern industrial cities, new ideas were gaining ground and economic prospects were opening up for many with such things as electrical and car factories and service industries growing rapidly alongside the familiar 19th Century bases of British industry. New ideas were taking root among people who were increasingly open to American culture with its meritocratic emphasis – from log cabin to White House – which showed that in one society at least what you could do was more important than who you were. British cinema audiences (some twenty million tickets were sold each week in the 1930s) watched films in which Americans seemed to live successful lives without encountering the social barriers which they saw around themselves. In Britain, aspirations could run up against well-established social norms in which who you were and where you had been educated were important considerations. Most of Britain's ruling élites, in politics, financial institutions, big business and, of course the officer corps of the armed forces, were the products of the public schools. In Victorian times they had educated those who would run the Empire and were seen as producing men best fitted for such an honourable task and this had not changed much by the 1930s. In the words of John Slessor, writing after the war, they were believed to produce the best leaders of men. The grammar schools (and I am using that term here as a shorthand for all forms of secondary education outside the public schools) could be relied upon to turn out decent citizens educated to fill the middle and lower management roles required by society but it was not seen as part of their job to turn out leaders. As a highly technical service the RAF depended on the outputs of the public and other secondary schools for most of its manpower and the RAFVR was to be no exception.

The growing threats from fascism, including the attack on Abyssinia, and the Spanish Civil War, stimulated left-wing ideas in Britain. For example, the Left Book Club which was launched by the publisher Victor Gollancz in 1936, had attracted 50 000 members within eighteen months and was aiming at a target of 100 000. Its publications, which ranged from attacks on fascism to discussions of social inequalities, were read by a wide spectrum of British society. It has been claimed, with some justification, that the ideas which it promulgated lay behind the Labour victory in the 1945 election. Other persuasive social movements were afoot. The Peace Pledge Union of 1934 sponsored a Peace Ballot in 1935 which attracted 11.5 million votes and clearly appealed to many. As the Air Council noted with concern in 1937, pacifism was particularly strong in the universities and too well represented in the press for its liking.

The decade also saw world speed and distance records broken on land, water and in the air – things which appealed to young men of spirit. The National League of Airmen and the Air League of the British Empire (ALBE) were doing all they could to stimulate air-mindedness and the Department of Civil Aviation was giving generous subsidies to flying clubs to help them get more young men and women into the air. However, even with such subsidies, flying as a sport was too expensive for the sort of men the RAFVR was aimed at. To conclude this brief synopsis of social mood indicators I can do no better than to give the last word to Lord Swinton. Chairing an Air Council debate about the effects of army recruitment on the RAF he commented that the old incentives to join up – the conscription of hunger and the desire to see the world – had been overtaken by the fact that, 'the majority of men already enjoy a life crowded with excitement'. It is against this sort of background that the RAFVR emerged.

Tedder's Role.

By 1936 it was clear that the leapfrogging series of Expansion Plans for the RAF which commenced in 1934 were calling for a larger number of pilots than could be produced by the existing sources of supply. Recruitment into the regular Service had to be vigorously supplemented by direct entry reserves. Leaving aside the AAF and the University Air Squadrons (UAS), the existing direct entry reserves consisted of Classes AA1 and AA2 of the RAFO and Class F for airmen pilots. With the exception of Cranwell cadets all *ab initio* training for pilots took place in the Elementary and Reserve Flying Training Schools (ERFTS) of which there were thirteen in 1935, after which a man progressed to a Service Flying Training School. The ERFTSs were civilian based organisations run by firms, such as De Havilland at Hatfield and Marshalls at Cambridge. They were under contract to the Air Ministry and provided an environment which mirrored Service attitudes. Attendance at an ERFTS was a full time affair so that, for example, a man joining Class F would have to leave his employment for a period of up to eight weeks during which he would put in 50 hours of flying training and associated ground instruction. After that he could return to his civilian job but he would need a further period of release later in the year in which to put in 20 hours of consecutive flying work. These calls for periods of full-time commitment were difficult to meet from an employer's point of view, since demands on industry were growing as re-armament programmes got under way. Lord Weir, a prominent industrialist co-opted onto the Air Council, pointed to this difficulty and remarked that under such circumstances firms were unlikely to let their best men have the necessary time off. A reserve capable of attracting large numbers of men would have to avoid the obvious difficulties of the Class F scheme. Yet, in 1936 an attempt was made to provide a reserve stop-gap before the RAFVR came on stream with a proposal for One Year Reservists – an adaptation of Class F which, of course, suffered from all its drawbacks in a magnified way and was soon abandoned.

Planning for the new reserve took place in AMP's Department where Air Cdre Arthur Tedder was Director of Training at the time. In February 1936, W L Scott, a senior civil servant in S7, the branch of the Air Ministry Secretariat which served AMP, put forward a paper incorporating the radical ideas which were being discussed within the Department, together with some of his own. It contained proposals which explicitly took account of social attitudes in the mid-1930s. The intention was to convey a clear message that whilst there was an educational hurdle to be surmounted there were to be no social barriers for reservists to cross. The educational requirements mirrored those for a Short Service Commission and specified attendance at either public or other secondary schools with achievement approximately up to the standard required for the School Certificate of the Oxford and Cambridge Examination Board. In practice, the term secondary school proved to be a catch-all which included not only the familiar grammar school but also a great variety of places where men could get themselves up to the required standards by part-time or evening study – for example in what were known as continuation schools and the night schools run by technical colleges. The reserve was to be taken to the men by making it as easy as possible for them to train whilst living at home and pursuing their normal civilian occupations. To counter the climate of pacifism, the sporting aspects of flying were to be emphasised in recruiting campaigns.

The main credit for the establishment of the RAFVR must certainly go to Tedder. Although he was critical of some aspects of Scott's paper he recognised that the new reserve should not be connected, like the AAF, to the County Territorial Associations. He thought that the Associations were 'moribund' and he knew that the links between the reserve and the public must be based on the active interests of young men of the middle classes in the broadest possible definition of that term. Scott wrote that the intention was to recruit from 'the poorer secondary school boys to the boys from the more expensive public schools. Youths from this wide social range have got to work together in the air and on the ground and to mix in social intercourse.'

With such aims in mind the AAF was not a good model for the RAFVR. Founded in 1924 it was composed of volunteers who flew at weekends and in their spare time but there any resemblance to what Tedder or Scott were thinking about came to an abrupt end. The AAF was organised in squadrons which were formed on a city or county basis. All its pilots were commissioned and it was characterised by the most extreme kind of social exclusiveness to be found in the Britain of the 1920s and '30s. To be an AAF pilot was to belong to a jealously guarded élite, access to which was barred by social and financial hurdles which were impassable for many who might have wished to fly with them. For example, a 1938 committee of enquiry, referred to later in this paper, found that the annual cost of belonging to the AAF as an officer could reach £50 per annum. A place as a day-boy at St Paul's, one of the most eminent of English public schools, could be had for £45 per annum in the 1930s. The RAFVR net was being designed to snare a much wider variety of fish.

In 1936, Air Cdre Chamier of the ALBE was arguing in favour of a reserve based on the flying clubs – without firm military commitment –which he described as a 'citizens air force' and which eventually saw the light of day in the shape of the Civil Air Guard. Wilfrid Freeman commented that peacetime pacifists tended to become wartime patriots – it required less courage – but Tedder would have none of that. For him, the ethos and discipline of the reserve should be tied to those of the RAF and reservists should have a full commitment to serve from the start. Entry was to be in the rank of AC2 with promotion to sergeant on the following day. Commissions were to be available to all who subsequently proved their worth, and on entry for some with appropriate aptitudes and previous flying experience, such as former and current UAS or RAFO members. Tedder initially had doubts about RAFVR officers rising from the ranks but eventually conceded the point. The AHB Narrative on the RAFVR claims that the decision to enrol men as sergeants, rather than as officers, reflects a clear choice between the public school man who might have expected a commission on entry and the secondary school chap who would not, in favour of the much larger contingent of the latter in the population. In practice the RAFVR came to contain men from the wide range of educational background which had been envisaged in its planning – from the universities and public schools to council elementary schools backed up with night school study. It was also the case that amalgamating the new reserve with the Service, which was a major principle of Tedder's thinking, was easier in the case of sergeants than it might have been with officers. The important point to bear in mind here is the large size of the new reserve which was anticipated.

The figure tends to vary a bit, depending on which document you are consulting at the PRO, but a round figure of five thousand RAFVR pilots on the books by September 1939 is respectable. Blending such a large number with a peacetime Service called for the exercise of some skill. A military unit is made up of men combining two kinds of quality, compatibility and competence. Competence is always required but the balance between the two Cs has to be carefully adjusted, especially in the case of officers who expect to share their lives with men who appreciate their outlook on life and know how to fit in. Too liberal an opening of the officer corps in peacetime to the men of a mass reserve would have presented compatibility problems on a big scale. For the AAF compatibility was a high priority – which is one of the reasons why it was never up to its established strength and why any prospect of getting involved with the RAFVR frightened it off. In spite of Air Ministry pressure it refused point-blank to help in training the new reserve. In January 1938 the AAF was running at only 51% of its peacetime establishment of pilots. Following a committee of enquiry chaired by the Under Secretary of State (Harold Balfour) into this matter it was forced to begin – in the face of opposition from among its squadrons – to train some of its own non-commissioned ground and aircrew members as pilots to compensate for the shortfall in its officer numbers. Even so it entered the war still seriously below its established strength. In wartime the balance shifts and competence assumes a more prominent place in the order of things. The pre-war RAFVR has to be seen primarily in competence terms. However, there are tales which relate how regular sergeants, who had spent years attaining that rank, were not exactly pleased to see men who had walked in off the streets wearing three stripes, and some first-hand accounts of frosty receptions given to RAFVR sergeants and officers when they were posted in to some AAF and RAF squadrons on the outbreak of war.

Getting off the ground.

Flying training was modelled on AAF practice using weekends and evenings coupled with short summer camps – but who would provide it, since the existing ERFTSs were not geographically local for the majority

By mid-1938 the schools training VR pilots were beginning to operate relatively heavy and powerful aeroplanes like this Hind – and, on occasion, as here, they had even begun to do it in the dark.

of the population? Could flying clubs be used for the purpose? Tedder was not in favour of that and preferred to work on the ERFTS model which he had been instrumental in founding in 1934 by inviting firms to tender for contracts to provide flying training on a weekend and evening basis at what were to be known as Aerodrome Centres which often shared space with a local flying club. In fact in December 1937 such Aerodrome Centres became designated as ERFTSs but I shall continue to use the former term for them in this paper.

It was never intended to provide a second-class route to pilot status in order to solve the numbers problem. That would be tackled by the device of opening up access to men who would otherwise have stood no chance of learning to fly. The RAFVR was not organised as squadrons so there was the problem of creating an *ésprit de corps* among its members. This was tackled by the use of Town Centres, which were to be set up in towns and cities close to the aerodromes. Ground instruction would be given in them but they were also to provide a social venue with the sort of recreational and sporting facilities which might be found in a club. Finding suitable premises was not easy, with a lot of bureaucracy at both national and local level to be dealt with but in spite of such trials the Air Ministry was successful in establishing a solid core of decent premises. The organisational tasks of negotiating the necessary contracts with firms, setting up both aerodrome and town centres and finding the large number of flying instructors and aircraft required should not be underestimated. The Air Ministry's vision in creating the new reserve was matched by the vigour which it applied to getting it into the air.

Treasury approval for the RAFVR was obtained in July 1936 but there were some delays in getting money released for flying training which had their effects in an interim period between January and April 1937. The intention was to begin recruiting in December 1936 but the first batch of fifty men was attested in January 1937; fourteen of them became pilots in the Battle of Britain. Between January and April 1937 men had to spend a full-time period at an existing ERFTS before returning home to continue training at a local airfield. This procedure resembled that of Class F and ran counter to the intention to provide training close to home without time off work. Insufficient ERFTSs were in a financial position to accommodate the new reservists in January but sufficient had come on stream by April to enable the planned mode of working to commence and by October there were nineteen of them in operation. The majority of reservists followed this weekend and evening route. Weather permitting, they had to attend aerodrome centres on alternate weekends – or put in the equivalent time during the week – and went to town centres for ground instruction on weekday evenings. There was a compulsory fifteen-day period of continuous training annually. However, these were minimum requirements and one big advantage of the scheme was its flexibility. The aerodrome centres were open every day so men could put in additional attendances if they were able to. It was certainly in the interest of the firms running the centres to encourage as much attendance as possible since their income was related to the number of flying hours they produced. After Munich, some who had reached an appropriate stage of training were required to spend a period of attachment to an RAF squadron – which in practice ranged from a few weeks to as long as six months. Late in 1938 AMP noted with satisfaction that around 50% of employers approached had proved willing to allow such periods of release to their men. Not everyone who joined the VR proved able to fly of course and, for those who didn't make it as pilots, re-mustering as observers and other categories of aircrew was possible as an alternative to leaving the scheme altogether.

If the question is posed, 'how many hours did VR pilots have in their log books by September 1939?' the answer would be about as simple to obtain as untangling a very large helping of spaghetti and measuring the length of each strand. It would all depend on when·they joined and how well they had been able to respond to opportunities to go beyond the minimum requirements laid down. Each reservist was expected to do sixty hours flying per annum, with twenty-eight coming from weekends, twelve from summer evenings and twenty from the annual camp. No doubt many did a lot more but there is no way of quantifying that without consulting personal records and they are not in the public domain. However, from personal correspondence, I know of men who had several hundred hours in their log books including experience on Tiger Moths, Magisters, Hinds, Harts and Audaxes. So, even in the absence of hard data, I think it would be absolutely safe to say that a lot of RAFVR pilots were not wet behind the ears when war broke out, although they may well have been in need of experience on more advanced Service types. The Phoney War provided valuable breathing space to allow them to get up to speed.

Finally, we can note that although its main focus was on creating a reserve of pilots the RAFVR was intended to recruit observers from the start. Frederick Bowhill thought that the name observer should be changed to navigator, which he saw as more attractive to potential recruits – and their girl friends. However, it was not until November 1938 that such recruitment started – rather late in the day it has to be said, since observers cannot be trained overnight and too few were produced by the outbreak of war. Wireless operators, air gunners and groundcrew were also directly recruited after November 1938 and by May 1939 the RAFVR contained 4394 aircrew, of whom 790 were not pilots. By July 1939 thirty-eight aerodrome and town centres were in operation and these figures had risen to forty-five aerodrome and forty-two town centres by September.

In Retrospect.

Why did men join the RAFVR and was all the time, effort and expense devoted to it by the Air Ministry and themselves repaid in the end? Men joined for a mixture of reasons. In its early days a big motive must have been the golden opportunity it offered to young men of small means to learn to fly. It would attract some with interests in aeroplanes as wonderful pieces of machinery. As the threat from Germany grew the motive of patriotism, which was always present, would increasingly dominate the decision to join. The Military Training Act of May 1939 (the first introduction of peacetime conscription in British history) did not result in any immediate call-up but it helped to focus the minds of young men on the looming possibility of active service. Those who wanted to ensure a place in the air for themselves in any conflict rapidly swelled the ranks of the RAFVR after that date. But was it all really worth it? I will end by quantifying the contribution of the RAFVR to Fighter Command in the Battle of Britain in the accompanying tables and by saying here that its pilots shot down at least 500 enemy aircraft during it.

It is clear that the contribution was a significant one. I must apologise to the far greater number of pre-war reservists who flew in other Commands – or who served on the ground as tradesmen or in the Medical, Equipment, Dental, Meteorological and Administrative and Special Duties Branches of the pre-war RAFVR which were established. I am not overlooking them; I simply do not have the necessary statistical data. Compiling such data would be an onerous, but worthwhile, task for someone else interested in the history of the RAFVR to undertake and I suspect that the results would echo Dowding when, in his desperate need for pilots in August 1940, he is reported to have exclaimed 'Thank God for the RAFVR'.

Sources:
PRO AIR2/2586, AIR6/23-40, AIR6/43-58, AIR32/14, AIR32/15, AIR41/65 and the ORBs of Battle of Britain accredited squadrons in the AIR27 collection. I would like to thank the fifty pre-war RAFVR Battle of Britain pilots who have given me information or have made helpful comments on this article, in particular; Air Cdre C B Brown, Flt Lt P R Hairs, Sqn Ldr I Hutchinson, Sqn Ldr K N T Lee, Flt Lt A C Leigh, Flt Lt J Pickering, and Capt A R F Thompson.

MODE OF ENTRY (REGULARS)	NUMBER IN BATTLE	KIA	SCORED	BATTLE 'ACES'
Cranwell	87	24	42	10
Direct Entry Permanent Commissions	17	4	8	1
Short Service Commissions	667	142	333	62
Halton Apprentices	117	22	52	8
Aircrafthands	48	9	15	2
Direct Entry Airmen Pilots	30	3	14	3
MODE OF ENTRY (RESERVES)				
AAF	153	28	74	10
RAFO	11	1	5	2
UAS[1]	97	23	37	3
AAF Ground/Air Crew	30	8	10	2
RAFVR[2]	782	135	242	21
OTHER SOURCES OF PILOTS				
European Air Forces	270	42	102	12
Dominion Air Forces	66	4	18	2
Fleet Air Arm	57	9	9	2

Fig 1. Analysis of pilots participating in the Battle of Britain.

Notes (to Fig 1):

[1] The 97 UAS members made their way into the AAF (11), RAFVR (71), Short Service Commissions (5), Direct Entry Permanent Commissions (8) whilst two retained RAFO commissions. Those killed in action, and/or Scored or became Battle Aces are included in the relevant Mode of Entry figures.

[2] 756 were pre-war entrants.

CATEGORY/RANK	AIRCRAFTMEN	NCOs	OFFICERS	TOTAL	KIA
Air Gunner	2	222	67	291	31
WOp/Air Gunner	-	93	-	93	11
Radar Operator	75	22	1	98	9
Observer	1	66	34	101	11
Totals	78	403	102	583	62

MODES OF ENTRY	RAF	AAF	Pre-War RAFVR	War Entry RAFVR	Total
	133	54	167	229	583

Fig 2. Analysis of aircrew, other than pilots, participating in the Battle of Britain.

Tables from Tony Mansell, 'Who Were the Few?', 1940, Issue 1 (Battle of Britain Memorial Trust; 2001). Scorers with confirmed whole or part claims have been identified from K G Wynn, *Men of the Battle of Britain* (Selsdon; 2000). Battle Aces are those achieving five or more confirmed whole claims during the Battle identified from C Shores and C Williams, *Aces High* (London; 1994) and C Shores, *Aces High*, Vol II (London; 1999). No account has been taken of probables or damaged claims. Any errors in the Scored or Battle Aces columns are my own.

THE AUXILIARY AIR FORCE IN WW II

Christopher Shores

Christopher Shores is, or was, a Chartered Surveyor by profession but he has been writing on aviation history for many years, his first hardback appearing as long ago as 1966. There have been many more since, and there are more to come now that he given up his day job. The range of topics that he has tackled is remarkably broad but he is singularly well-versed in the operational history of the RAF in WW II and his Aces High *is the standard reference work on the achievements of its fighter pilots.*

Before I was invited to speak about 'the auxiliaries' and their squadrons, I find on looking back that my perceptions were probably precisely those which many interested in the history of the Royal Air Force have had since the war.

Despite being involved in the study of British fighter aviation for the past forty years or so, my immediate reaction was that the auxiliary units had proved to be a vital part of Fighter Command's strength in 1940 and that those essentially 'weekend' pilots produced some of the most impressive results of the fighting during the Battle of Britain throughout the summer and autumn of that year.

Yes, I would have added, they were leavened with the odd regular, and reinforced by some of the new VR boys but, essentially, it was the auxiliaries who made up a sizeable proportion of the available defences.

As I have looked in depth into the subject in preparation for today's deliberations, I find that my initial reaction was not entirely sustainable, which has come as more than something of a shock to me. Have I been 'set up' to act as executioner of fondly-held pre-conceptions, I even found myself asking?

To answer this question I am about to present you with some quite detailed statistics which I have prepared. Now I know that there are 'lies, damned lies, and statistics', but in practice carefully prepared, and hopefully unslanted, statistical evidence can often disabuse long-held beliefs based upon publicity, propaganda and the release of only partial information. I shall also suggest one or two avenues from which such misleading, partially misleading or overstated impressions may have emerged.

Jeff Jefford has summarised the formation and development of the AAF prior to September 1939, so I shall not dwell on this period. Suffice to say that between May 1925 and March 1939 twenty-one squadrons had been formed and one disbanded. Between July 1934 and August 1939 fourteen of these squadrons had become fighter units.

With the outbreak of war in September 1939, and prior to their first experience of action, these fourteen squadrons were equipped, or were shortly to be equipped, as follows:

Hawker Hurricanes – Nos 501, 504, 601 and 605 Sqns
Gloster Gladiators – Nos 607 and 615 Sqns
Bristol Blenheim Ifs – Nos 600 and 604 Sqns
Supermarine Spitfires – Nos 602, 603, 609, 610, 611 and 616 Sqns

Of the other AAF units, Nos 500, 502, 608 and 612 Sqns were to operate under the control of Coastal Command, equipped in the main with Avro Ansons for coastal and anti-submarine patrol work, whilst Nos 613 and 614 Sqns had been earmarked for army co-operation duties.

At this stage, as the AAF was being mobilised, all units were undoubtedly at their most 'pure' as 'auxiliary' squadrons – even if, as Jeff Jefford has pointed out, most were well below establishment, particularly in pilot strengths. Certainly, however, their groundcrew personnel were essentially those who had faithfully served their chosen units throughout much of the 1930s, and who were all enlisted under provisions which allowed them, as AAF personnel, to refuse a posting to any other unit – at least for the remaining years of their AAF engagements.

Amongst the pilots, however, this situation was not always the case. Selection policies, certainly by some of the squadrons, had been tightly restricted to those whose social standing was considered suitable for immediate commissioned service, and who it was felt would integrate easily with the officers already serving with the unit. This has led since to the conception that AAF units were socially exclusive to a point of downright snobbishness, and that some were little more than 'rich men's flying clubs'. I am sure that some of you will have heard 'Johnny' Johnson wax lyrical regarding his own lack of acceptability when seeking to join one such squadron, upon the discovery that he did not hunt!

Certainly, there does seem to be some justification for the accusations made, although such criticisms must be tempered by recalling the very different social mores which were acceptable in those now quite far off and very different times.

The result, however, was undoubtedly to restrict access to the AAF and to cause many otherwise suitable young men to look instead to the more recently formed Volunteer Reserve.

With the replacement of the two-seat Demons by single-seat fighters in most of the squadrons chosen for such duties during the months preceding and during the early weeks of the war, the demand for air gunners was reduced, although the majority of these had in any event been in the main volunteers from amongst the ground crews, rather than dedicated aircrew personnel.

For most of the pre-war period the auxiliary squadrons had kept their pilot establishment resolutely of an all-officer nature. It required considerable pressure from the Air Ministry before they were obliged to accept the concept of a proportion of that establishment being made up of NCO pilots. Consequently a few – a very few – suitable applicants from the existing ground personnel were accepted and trained as pilots with the squadrons in time for the war.

It had long been the norm for each squadron to incorporate one or two regular officers, who usually acted as flying instructors and/or adjutants, maintaining the units outside the periods when the volunteers were available for duty.

As war approached, for the reasons of selection that I have set out, and due to the alternative availability of the VR, not all squadrons were by any means at full establishment, and numbers of regulars were posted in to bring them up to strength, particularly filling Flight Commander posts where a greater degree of experience was desirable. As soon as VR entrants, also called up with the outbreak of hostilities, completed their training, they too began to be posted to the auxiliary units in quite considerable numbers. However, since few VRs were sufficiently trained for immediate squadron service, it was the spring and early summer of 1940 before many of these personnel began to make their presence felt.

It also needs to be said that some of these young men, particularly those emanating from the University Air Squadrons and commissioned upon completion of their flying training, may well have proved acceptable entrants to the auxiliary units under their old recruitment policies had the onset of war not intervened.

It is here that I must reiterate that my main interest has, over the years, been fighter pilots, units and operations. Whilst I shall be saying something more regarding those units which did not become involved in such activities, it is essentially upon the fighter units that I shall now largely dwell. Certainly it was in this role that the auxiliaries were to gain their main fame.

Why does my interest lie in this direction? Well, I'm a frustrated would-be fighter pilot myself, and I find the ethos and character of the genre to be interesting and attractive.

With the outbreak of war two auxiliary squadrons, Nos 607 and 615, both of which you will recall were equipped with Gladiators, were despatched to France to form part of the Air Component of the British Expeditionary Force. Leavened with some regulars, it was still too early for these units to have been reinforced to any substantial extent by VRs. However, the 'Phoney War' provided them with little opportunity to do other than undertake training until the spring of 1940. Such activity as there was for British fighter squadrons in the skies over France at this time tended to devolve on the regular units of the Advanced Air Striking Force, based further south.

It was over Scotland and the far north of England that auxiliary units were to be amongst the first fighters of the RAF to see action, as they intercepted *Luftwaffe* bombers and reconnaissance aircraft appearing over the naval bases in the Firth of Forth and at Scapa Flow. Thus it was the Spitfires of Nos 602 and 603 Sqns which first drew blood for the AAF, joined early in 1940 by No 605 Sqn, posted north to assist in the defence of Scapa.

The onset of the German offensive into France, Belgium and Holland which commenced on 10 May 1940, found Nos 607 and 615 Sqns completing conversion to Hurricanes, so that they were at least spared the experience of having to contest the might of the *Luftwaffe* in elderly biplanes.

Plans for the reinforcement of both the Air Component and the AASF were already in place, and on this first day No 501 Sqn flew over to join the fray, followed two days later by No 504 Sqn. No 501 Sqn was wholly different from most of the other auxiliary units, its Special Reserve origins perhaps having led to the unit's fielding a far greater preponderance of VR pilots than did most of its fellow units, whilst the proportion of AAF pilots was extremely low.

As the fighting, both in the air and on the ground, became desperate, more squadrons were sent out, whilst other units despatched flights to operate from airfields on the Continent for a day or two at a time, returning to bases in southern England with the onset of evening; one of these was 'A' Flight of No 601 Sqn, which arrived at Merville on 16 May.

As the German advance neared the English Channel, No 504 Sqn, having suffered rather heavy losses, was withdrawn to England on the 20th. Home-based squadrons were now increasingly to enter the action, and on the 21st No 605 Sqn flew down from Wick in Scotland to be one of those involved.

With Belgium now out of the conflict and northern France being overrun, the Air Component squadrons, including Nos 607 and 615, were also withdrawn to England, only No 501 Sqn remaining with the AASF further south – the sole auxiliary unit still on the Continent. Indeed, this squadron was to soldier on there for several more weeks, finally withdrawing to the Channel Islands on 19 June, and from there back to England, having achieved the outstanding auxiliary record of the Battle of France.

Meanwhile, with the BEF and a substantial element of the French Army hemmed in at the Channel coast, the great evacuation from the Dunkirk area commenced. In support, 11 Group of Fighter Command at last threw in its carefully husbanded Spitfires, which became increasingly involved from 21 May onwards. From the 27th Nos 609, 610, 611 and 616 Sqns all saw their first action here. Indeed, by the end of June all of the auxiliary fighter squadrons had been 'blooded' in France or over the Channel, with the exception of Nos 602 and 603 Sqns in Scotland, which, as we have seen, had already been in action against intruders in the north. This even included the Blenheim-equipped Nos 600 and 604 Sqns, which had undertaken some patrol activity, although 600 had paid dearly on the first day of the *Blitzkrieg* when they flew up to the Dutch coast to attack German transport aircraft which were landing there.

With the conclusion of the Dunkirk evacuation, and of the residual operations over France during the remainder of June 1940, a balance could be drawn to assess the results and costs to date. See Figure 1.

Whilst aircraft were replaceable, the fifty-eight pilots lost (five of the aircrew noted as having been lost by No 600 Sqn had actually been air gunners), of whom perhaps at best the ten wounded or injured might be expected to return to their units to fly again, were irreplaceable where

Unit	Claims		Losses			
	Confirmed	Unconfirmed	Aircraft	Pilots* Killed	Pilots* Wounded	Pilots* PO
No 501 Sqn	51	9	5	3	0	0
No 607 Sqn	41	16	13	6	2	2
No 615 Sqn	17	11	11	4	3	2
No 601 Sqn	15	4	11	1	1	0
No 610 Sqn	12	3	8	7	0	0
No 605 Sqn	8	6	10	4	1	2
No 504 Sqn	8	5	11	4	3	1
No 609 Sqn	8	4	5	4	0	0
No 616 Sqn	7	5	2	1	0	0
No 611 Sqn	1	4	2	2	0	0
No 604 Sqn	1	0	0	0	0	0
No 600 Sqn	0	0	5	10	0	0
Totals	**169**	**67**	**83**	**46**	**10**	**7**

*Strictly speaking, five of these men were actually Blenheim air gunners.

Fig 1. Claims versus losses for AAF fighter squadrons to the end of June 1940.

---

11 Group (Southern England)

17 squadrons of Hurricanes (including Nos 501,601 and 615 Sqns)
8 squadrons of Spitfires (including Nos 609 and 610 Sqns)
4 squadrons of Blenheim Ifs (including Nos 600 and 604 Sqns)
1 squadron of Gladiators

12 Group (East Midlands)

3 squadrons of Hurricanes
5 squadrons of Spitfires (including No 611 Sqn)
2 squadrons of Blenheim Ifs
1 squadron of Defiants

13 Group (Scotland and Northern England)

9 squadrons of Hurricanes (including Nos 504, 605 and 607 Sqns)
6 squadrons of Spitfires (including Nos 602, 603 and 616 Sqns)
1 squadron of Defiants

Fig 2. Deployment of Fighter Command in early July 1940.

they had been auxiliaries, other than by other categories of personnel, since there was no effective reserve of specifically 'auxiliary' pilots.

Coupled with the wastage normal during such sustained operational flying by way of accidents, and by certain of the longer-serving auxiliaries proving to be rather 'long in the tooth' to continue in this manner, by the start of July 1940 the number of immediately available AAF pilots in the fourteen fighter squadrons had already been significantly reduced.

So it is that we reach the critical point at the start of July 1940 when the United Kingdom, standing alone, prepared to meet the onslaught of the *Luftwaffe* in all its fury upon the home islands. At this stage Fighter Command had some fifty-seven squadrons available, deployed as at Figure 2.

By November 1940 the number of Groups had been expanded to six, 9 Group having taken over the north west of England, 10 Group the south west, and 14 Group the far north of Scotland. Available units had increased by six squadrons and two flights of Hurricanes – although, obviously, by no further AAF units.

Unit	AAF	RAF	RAFVR	Foreign	Total
No 501 Sqn	4 (2)	20 (8)	32 (12)	11 (5)	67
No 504 Sqn	7 (4)	8 (3)	9 (3)	0 (0)	24
No 601 Sqn	20 (12)	12 (8)	19 (3)	4 (1)	55
No 602 Sqn	10 (9)	7 (7)	15 (10)	0 (0)	32
No 603 Sqn	9 (8)	13 (12)	17 (10)	1 (1)	40
No 605 Sqn	7 (1)	11 (4)	14 (6)	3 (2)	35
No 607 Sqn	10 (5)	6 (2)	12 (3)	9 (2)	37
No 609 Sqn	11 (5)	11 (11)	14 (5)	4 (1)	40
No 610 Sqn	13 (6)	16 (6)	35 (9)	0 (0)	64
No 611 Sqn	9 (4)	11 (5)	20 (2)	0 (0)	40
No 615 Sqn	14 (6)	18 (6)	19 (5)	5 (0)	56
No 616 Sqn	9 (9)	11 (6)	16 (2)	0 (0)	36
Totals	**123 (71)**	**145 (78)**	**221 (70)**	**37 (12)**	**526**
% of Total	**23.4%**	**27.6%**	**42%**	**7%**	

Fig 3. *Analysis, by entry type, of pilots entitled to wear the Battle of Britain clasp who flew with nominally AAF single-seat fighter squadrons between July and December 1940.*

It is now, therefore, that I am going to bombard you with statistics. I am afraid that the lists are inevitably going to be a bit busy but they will be reproduced in the Journal so you will be able to study them at your leisure in due course.

Figure 3 reflects those personnel entitled to wear the Battle of Britain clasp who served in one of the AAF units during the period July-December 1940, related to their respective squadrons. These figures do *not*, however, include pilots who flew no operational sorties during the period under review, nor those who joined their squadrons during December. Thus the number of VR personnel may be slightly understated, although I do not believe to any significant degree.

You will note that the numbers of pilots serving with particular squadrons differ quite considerably. This is a good indication of the extent to which the unit in question was involved in action. Comparing the 'throughput' of pilots at Figure 3 with the totals of claims and losses in a later table, it quickly becomes apparent which units bore the brunt of the fighting. Again, some squadrons which suffered substantial casualties in a short period, or otherwise proved to be less effective than others, were frequently moved away to the north and classified as 'C' squadrons, whereby they became little more than glorified advanced operational training units, bringing the green young VRs up to a rather better state of preparedness before feeding them into the units in the south.

Thus quite a number of those who make up the totals I list, actually served in more than one unit during the period under review. Relatively few served continuously with one squadron throughout the period, although a number certainly did.

On reflection, Figure 3 is most revealing. Not one AAF unit enjoyed a preponderance of AAF pilots on its strength during the second half of 1940. Indeed only in No 601 Sqn, perhaps the archetypal AAF unit, did they even form the predominant group. In eight of the squadrons they were outnumbered not only by the VRs, but by the regulars as well, all of whom were of similar pre-war vintage. In every unit, except No 601 Sqn, the VRs proved to be the predominant number, and indeed, in No 501 Sqn, apparently the archetypal VR unit (although in fact outstripped by No 610 Sqn), the auxiliaries were even outnumbered by the foreign pilots who reached the unit during the summer and autumn.

You will also notice that I have included a further figure in brackets alongside all of the above figures with the exception of the final column of totals. Since the primary job of a fighter pilot, particularly when flying in defence of his country, is to shoot down the aircraft of the opposing side, these figures indicate the numbers of pilots who made claims for shooting down, or sharing in shooting down, enemy aircraft, for which they received confirmation.

I believe that these percentages are extremely high compared with the situation appertaining to the rest of the RAF's fighter activities during the war. This is undoubtedly due to several factors: the ready availability of many targets; the presence of large numbers of bomber aircraft, which required less skill in deflection shooting to bring down; and the circumstances in which Fighter Command was operating, ie over its own territory, rather than over a hostile environment.

Since success in aerial combat contains a mixture of innate skill, training, experience, opportunity and downright luck, it is perhaps a good indication of the AAF's state of training and experience that no less than

57.7% of those engaged in the Battle of Britain (71 of 123) were able to submit confirmable claims. It may, of course, also be because, by and large, they were with the squadrons for a longer period than those regulars and VRs posted in as reinforcements during this time. Many of the regulars were already with the units in July 1940, however, as were some of the VRs, but this factor can potentially 'skew' the results. Nonetheless, 53.8% of the regulars (78 of 145) were also able to 'connect' with their targets.

Given that many of the VRs reached their units with minimal training and less experience, I consider that the fact that nearly a third of them (31.7%) were able to make claims before the end of 1940, was significant – and praiseworthy. The apparently rather disappointing results achieved by the relatively small number of experienced Polish, Czech, French and Belgian personnel (32.4% able to claim) is surely explained by their relatively late arrival on the scene and the difficulties many undoubtedly encountered with language, tactics and unfamiliar equipment. The results that many were later able to achieve (or were already achieving) in the all-Polish and all-Czech units at this time, would certainly seem to support this.

Of course, simply being able to share in shooting down one or two bombers does not necessarily compare with a pilot who is able single-handed to account for ten or a dozen of the enemy. I have therefore prepared a further table (Figure 4) indicating how many victories were claimed by each category of pilots in each of the squadrons. It should be noted that, due to the presence of a considerable number of shared claims, the totals do not always add up precisely to the number of victories claimed by each unit. This problem is exacerbated by the inability to identify to whom eight of the victories listed for No 605 Sqn should be allocated. The figures in brackets relate to the number of claiming pilots identified in Figure 3.

Here, on average, the regulars were slightly ahead of the auxiliaries – but look at the performance of the VRs! The results mirror quite closely the numbers indicated in the previous table. Those of the two predominantly AAF units, Nos 601 and 602 Sqns, both show the auxiliaries claiming more victories than all the others, but only just; ignoring the shared claims we have No 601 Sqn with 32:32 and No 602 Sqn with 35:34. The biggest differential in favour of AAF pilots was actually achieved by No 615 Sqn with 25:20.

Unit	AAF	RAF	RAFVR	Foreign
No 501 Sqn	(2) 2	(8) 26 & 5 sh	(12) 42 & 1 sh	(5) 19 & 1 sh
No 504 Sqn	(4) 6 & 6 sh	(3) 7	(3) 3	–
No 601 Sqn	(12) 32 & 12 sh	(8) 24 & 6 sh	(3) 7 & 3 sh	(1) 1
No 602 Sqn	(9) 35 & 11 sh	(7) 5 & 5 sh	(10) 29 & 7 sh	–
No 603 Sqn	(8) 12 & 12 sh	(12) 33 & 7 sh	(10) 23 & 15 sh	(1) 1
No 605 Sqn	(1) 19 & 1 sh	(4) 12 & 8 sh	(6) 7 & 5 sh	(2) 3 & 2 sh
No 607 Sqn	(5) 2 & 5 sh	(2) 4 & 1 sh	(5) 20 & 2 sh	(2) 2
No 609 Sqn	(5) 23 & 3 sh	(11) 36 & 5 sh	(5) 20 & 2 sh	(1) 1
No 610 Sqn	(6) 17 & 2 sh	(6) 33 & 2 sh	(6) 20 & 2 sh	–
No 611 Sqn	(4) 5 & 7 sh	(5) 5 & 4 sh	(2) 1 & 1 sh	–
No 615 Sqn	(6) 25 & 4 sh	(6) 16 & 2 sh	(5) 4 & 4 sh	–
No 616 Sqn	(9) 8 & 9 sh	(6) 14 & 6 sh	(2) 2	–
Totals	(71) 187 & 2 sh	(78) 215 & 40 sh	(70) 160 & 43 sh	(12) 26 & 3 sh
Average per Pilot	2.6 & 1 share	2.75 & 0.5 share	2.28 & 0.6 share	2.13 & 0.33

Fig 4. Analysis, by entry type, of victories claimed by the body of pilots represented by Figure 3.
sh = shared

Again, that archetypal VR unit, No 501 Sqn, presented figures at the opposite end of the spectrum – AAF 2, others 87! Eight other units showed significant success ratios in favour of the non-auxiliaries, notably:- No 603 Sqn at 12:57, No 609 Sqn at 23:57 and No 610 Sqn with 17:53.

But, as with all statistics, there is the 'maverick' that can produce a totally non-typical result, due to specific circumstances. The example here is No 605 Sqn, which presents a ratio of 19:22 – but all of those 19 were claimed by just *one* AAF pilot, Archie McKellar!

This is all very well of course, but it is now well-known and accepted that the claims made during the Battle of Britain exceeded German losses by a factor of a little over one third (2692 victories claimed as against 1733 actual losses). In considering the cost, and a cost:benefit analysis of what was achieved, it is perhaps necessary to reduce the claims made to about 60-65% of the total to compare with the *Luftwaffe's* actual losses. Which brings me to my final table, Figure 5.

On this rough 'rule of thumb' it may be shown that all but one of the AAF units did better than break even, perhaps demonstrating why the defence proved so successful. Even in the one unit which perhaps did not break even – No 607 Sqn – the deficit was marginal, and this was a squadron which had already achieved good results earlier in the year.

It is perhaps worth noting, however, that although the adjusted claim:loss ratio works out overall at nearly two (1.89) victories for each aircraft lost, these adjusted ratios differ quite markedly between the Hurricane and Spitfire squadrons. Hurricane units were apparently achieving 1.47 victories for each loss, whilst the Spitfires were getting 2.4 for each loss. These ratios are based upon my adjustments. Based upon the claims being made at the time, they *thought* that they were achieving respectively 2.33:1 and 3.8:1 (3:1 overall).

The other important question is how the AAF units had performed in comparison with the rest of Fighter Command's squadrons. The answer here is stunningly well. Out of about sixty squadrons taking part in the Battle, Nos 602 and 603 Sqns were the second and third highest scoring respectively. No 501 Sqn was placed fifth, No 609 Sqn seventh, 601 Sqn eleventh and 610 Sqn fourteenth. To have six squadrons amongst the fourteen most successful was without any doubt a most extraordinary performance.

| Unit | Losses | | | | Claims | |
| | Aircraft | Pilots | | | Unadjusted | Approx 60-65% |
		Killed	Wounded/Injured	POW		
No 501 Sqn	44	21	8	–	93	59
No 504 Sqn	5	4	–	–	21	13
No 601 Sqn	21	11	6	–	73 & 1 sh	46
No 602 Sqn	16	6	2	–	102	65
No 603 Sqn	34	15	13	1	98	62
No 605 Sqn	29	10	7	–	56 & 1 sh	35
No 607 Sqn	14	9	1	–	21	13
No 609 Sqn	13	9	1	–	90 & 1 sh	57
No 610 Sqn	25	9	8	–	71	45
No 611 Sqn	1	1	–	–	15	9
No 615 Sqn	16	5	8	–	36 & 1 sh	23
No 616 Sqn	18	7	6	1	31	19
Totals	**236**	**107**	**60**	**2**	**707 & 4 sh**	**446**

Fig 5. Claims versus losses for AAF fighter squadrons during the period July-December 1940.

Classic Battle of Britain period shot of one of No 615 Sqn's Hurricanes landing at Kenley.

Amongst individual pilots too, the record was impressive. No 501 Sqn's J H 'Ginger' Lacey – a VR pilot – was one of the two top-scorers of 1940, with twenty-three confirmed. Eight other pilots, four of them auxiliaries and four regulars, were amongst the fifty-to-sixty most successful. Amongst the auxiliaries, Archie McKellar (No 605 Sqn) with nineteen, John Dundas (No 609 Sqn) with twelve and four shared and Carl Davis (No 601 Sqn) with nine and one shared, were all killed before the end of the year. Only Finlay Boyd (No 602 Sqn) with eight and seven shared, survived. Amongst the four most successful regulars, however, all survived both the year and the war, this group being headed by Brian Carbury (No 603 Sqn) with fifteen and two shared, and John Ellis (No 610 Sqn) with twelve and one shared.

Following these successes, however, the end of 1940 virtually marked the end of the AAF as far as the twelve day fighter squadrons were concerned. The campaigns of 1940 had cost the lives in action of at least 153 pilots, with another nine having become prisoners for the duration and 70 more being wounded or injured, quite apart from the accidental losses which formed an integral part of training and sustained operational flying. Whilst many of these, particularly during the latter half of 1940, were not auxiliaries, this total operational loss averaged roughly nineteen per squadron. This is equivalent to about 100% of the initial pilot strength of each of the twelve AAF units.

Virtually every pilot who had served from the start of the war and who had survived, had been rested by the end of the year, worn out, or needed to pass on experience at the burgeoning Operational Training Units, or both. By the start of 1941 the products of the Commonwealth Air Training Plan were beginning to reach the UK, and increasingly fighter squadrons were to become manned by the VR, with the older, experienced pilots serving as Wing Leaders, Squadron and Flight Commanders. Whilst the old AAF squadrons retained their pre-war personalities and traditions for the time being, due to the continued presence of their groundcrews, Adjutants, Intelligence Officers, etc, in the air they were 'auxiliary' in name only.

The same did not, at this stage, apply to the two night fighter units, Nos 600 and 604 Sqns, which only now began to come into their own as the winter of 1940-41 saw them begin conversion from their ineffective Blenheims to the powerful new Beaufighter with the beginnings of reliable AI radar equipment. They were just in time, for the '*Blitz*' was now getting fully under way by night.

The AAF units serving with Coastal and Army Co-operation Commands had not suffered the wastage and exhaustion of the day fighters either, and they too were able to retain their essentially 'auxiliary' nature for a little longer. However, even here, as more effective equipment became available and operations intensified, the policy of implementing tours of duty for aircrew gradually caused the old auxiliaries to melt away, until by the end of 1941 and into 1942 these units too remained auxiliaries only with respect to those labouring to keep the aircraft aloft.

It is a matter of conjecture as to whether the 'heart' of a squadron rests with the aircrew or its ground personnel – probably an amalgam of the two. But once a squadron, the main purpose of which is *flying*, loses its aircrew element, its underlying nature must surely change.

Undoubtedly, the groundcrew remained fiercely proud and loyal to their squadrons. Whilst I have come across few, if any, examples of aircrew refusing promotions involving postings to other units, the same was not the case with those on the ground and, in time, this came to present the powers-that-be with some problems.

In some cases, as I shall detail later, squadrons lost their air parties on a permanent basis, but still the ground personnel were unwilling to be

One of No 611 Sqn's Spitfire VBs at Coltishall, winter 1943-44.

divided up and posted elsewhere, requiring new, and on occasion, totally different, types of air echelons to be grafted on to keep the old number plate going. If an auxiliary airman warranted a promotion which required his posting to another unit, he could refuse. Alternatively, if it was desirable to post in, say, an armourer corporal with the required experience, it could prove difficult to persuade an existing member of the squadron to be moved on, to maintain the appropriate establishment.

Most AAF ground personnel were on a four-year enlistment, however, the length of their remaining entitlement to *auxiliary* terms of service being governed by the date on which their current engagements had commenced – and in no case was this later than 1939. During 1942-43, therefore, it became possible to persuade most auxiliary airmen to co-operate by the veiled (or outright) threat that they would be discharged from the AAF on conclusion of their engagement and immediately conscripted into the VR, obliging them to have to start from scratch all over again. This was a prospect which soon brought all but the most recalcitrant into line.

So what became of the twenty AAF units during the rest of the war? In brief, they all continued to serve, in a variety of roles, for most of the rest of the period of hostilities but, although they were still identified by the noble auxiliary numbers and bore their pre-war titles, they became increasingly indistinguishable from all of the other squadrons fielded by the wartime RAF.

Amongst the day fighter units, Nos 501, 504, 602, 609, 610, 611 and 616 Sqns – soon all Spitfire-equipped – continued to be based in the UK, taking part in the continued defence of the country and in the costly sweeps, bomber escorts and other operations carried out over the coastal areas of occupied Europe between 1941 and 1943. Having incorporated a flight of Belgian pilots for some months, in 1942 No 609 Sqn converted to the powerful Typhoon, becoming involved in low altitude operations against 'hit-and-run' fighter-bombers along the south coast of England. Ultimately this unit was incorporated into the 2nd Tactical Air Force and became a rocket-firing ground support unit during the campaigns in Normandy and into Holland and Germany.

No 602 Sqn was also an early part of 2nd TAF, but operated Spitfire IXs in the air superiority role. It returned to the UK in September 1944 for home-based duties.

With the appearance of the V-1 flying bombs during June 1944, No 610 Sqn, newly-equipped with Griffon-engined Spitfire XIVs, took part in many interceptions of these missiles, joined in August by the first Gloster Meteor jet fighters to see action – in the hands of No 616 Sqn. No 501 Sqn re-equipped with Tempests late in 1944 to continue operations against the V-1s by night when they were being air-launched from He 111 bombers over the North Sea. The unit would be disbanded during April 1945.

Meanwhile, No 610 Sqn moved to Holland to join 2nd TAF during December 1944, but this unit too was to be disbanded at the start of March 1945.

Nos 600 and 604 Sqns continued their night defence duties throughout 1941-42, and indeed 604 was to do so for the rest of the war, re-equipping on the way with the splendid Mosquito. This unit also joined 2nd TAF in December 1944, but was disbanded in the following April. At the start of 1943, however, No 600 Sqn took its Beaufighters to Algeria to support the campaign in Tunisia, of which more later.

Towards the end of 1941 No 605 Sqn was despatched to the Middle East, the air party flying off an aircraft carrier to Malta during November. Some of the pilots plus the groundcrew, who were coming out by sea, were sent to the Far East following the Japanese attack in December. Here, during the later stages of the fighting in the Dutch East Indies, some of the surviving Hurricane pilots from other units were amalgamated with these elements to form a new No 605 Sqn on Java, but all were captured when the island fell to the Japanese in March 1942. Meanwhile, the squadron's original air echelon, which was still on Malta, was absorbed into other local fighter units. Subsequently a completely

A Beaufighter X of No 603 Sqn at Gambut in 1944 after the unit had been reconstituted for maritime strike ops in the Aegean.

new No 605 Sqn was formed in the UK in June 1942 to undertake night intruder operations with Havocs, later replaced by Mosquitos. This unit continued to undertake such operations for the rest of the war, moving to the Continent during its closing weeks.

During 1942 Malta continued to be under sustained siege. In April Nos 601 and 603 Sqns were brought up to strength, re-equipped with tropicalised Spitfire Vs, and flown off to the island from the American carrier, USS *Wasp*. They were not to be joined on the island by their ground elements, which travelled by sea round the Cape of Good Hope to Egypt. In June No 601 Sqn's pilots flew to Egypt, where, reunited with their ground party, the squadron became one of the first Spitfire units to operate over the Western Desert.

In the meantime, No 603 Sqn's air party had been merged with two new Spitfire squadrons which were being formed on Malta and for a time the unit effectively ceased to exist. The ground party had stuck together, however, and in 1943 they formed the nucleus of a new No 603 Sqn which operated maritime strike Beaufighters over the Aegean.

Following the Japanese attack, more reinforcements were required for the India-Burma front, and in March 1942 Nos 607 and 615 Sqns (together again!) were despatched to this theatre. Here they initially operated Hurricane IIs, but in September 1943 both were re-equipped with Spitfire Vs, some of the first to reach the Far East. In the spring of 1944 these were replaced with the latest Mark VIIIs which were

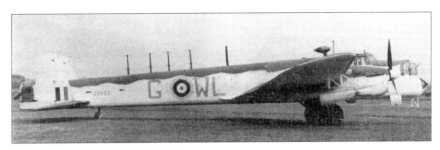

A Whitley VII of No 612 Sqn.

employed on air superiority and ground strafing duties throughout the rest of the fighting in Burma. In June 1945 No 615 Sqn was disbanded, its number plate promptly being re-allocated to No 135 Sqn, which was flying Thunderbolts.

In the Mediterranean area meanwhile, following the removal of the Axis from North Africa, Nos 600 and 601 Sqns comprised a part of the Desert Air Force, continuing respectively their night and day activities over Sicily and then Italy until the conclusion of the war. With the reduction of targets available in the Aegean area, the Beaufighter-equipped No 603 Sqn was disbanded in December 1944 and a further new unit of that identity (the third) was formed in the UK, equipped with Spitfire IXs, with which it was to specialise in dive-bombing attacks on V-2 launching sites during the closing months of the war.

Of the other, non-fighter, units, Nos 500, 502, 608 and 612 Sqns had continued to fly with Coastal Command, Nos 500 and 608 Sqns replacing their Ansons with Blenheims, and then with Hudsons, while the other two units received Whitleys. Late in 1942 612 exchanged these for Wellingtons, whilst at the start of 1943 No 502 Sqn received four-engined Halifaxes. So equipped, these two units would continue their anti-submarine patrols over the Bay of Biscay and the Atlantic for the rest of the war.

Late in 1942 Nos 500 and 608 Sqns were both posted to North Africa as a counter to U-boats operating in the Mediterranean. Meanwhile Nos 613 and 614 Sqns had seen little activity other than training and exercising with the army. No 613 Sqn had replaced its elderly Hector biplanes with Lysanders, which No 614 Sqn also flew. In July 1941 the latter unit received Blenheims for longer range reconnaissance work. At the end of 1942, however, it was redesignated as a bomber squadron and, equipped with the ill-fated Bisley (Blenheim V), also went to North Africa.

No 613 Sqn replaced its Lysanders with Tomahawks for the fighter-reconnaissance role in August 1941, but in April 1942 it received the much more effective Mustang I. In October 1943 the unit was reformed with Mosquito VI fighter-bombers for intruder work, continuing in this role until the end of the war as part of 2nd TAF.

In the Mediterranean area during 1944, lack of Axis activity in the main sea basin led to the disbandment of Nos 500, 608 and 614 Sqns. No 614 Sqn was the first to go in January, No 462 Sqn, Royal Australian Air Force, with Halifax heavy bombers then being renumbered as No 614. In July No 27 Sqn of the South African Air Force, a Baltimore light bomber unit, was renumbered as No 500 Sqn, while during the same month a new Mosquito squadron was formed in the UK to operate as a Pathfinder unit in the Light Night Striking Force of Bomber Command; this unit was assigned No 608 Sqn's number plate.

It may thus be seen that by the later months of the war the AAF had virtually ceased to exist, many of the squadrons operating during that period bearing no relationship to the original units of 1939-40 other than to carry the same number plates within a vastly expanded air force.

Nevertheless, while it may be stretching a point to claim the later exploits of these units as 'auxiliary' battle honours, that does not mean that AAF personnel were not continuing to exert an influence on the later conduct of the war. We might well ask, therefore, what service did some of the more notable survivors of the great days of 1940 continue to give? The answer is that this was not inconsiderable. About a dozen of them survived the war with the rank of group captain (equivalent to one from each day fighter squadron). Amongst them was John Cunningham, who had been No 604 Sqn's outstanding night fighter pilot during 1941. He ended the war as one of the RAF's three most successful night fighters, although it must be said that he was the only auxiliary to become a high scorer at this 'trade'. Max Aitken had also become a night fighter, but finished the war commanding one of Coastal Command's Strike Wings of Mosquitos and Beaufighters.

George 'Sheep' Gilroy and Hugh 'Cocky' Dundas both became notable Wing Leaders, as did Finlay Boyd and all ended up commanding fighter wings, the first two in Italy and the third in Burma. Walter Churchill achieved a similar position on Malta as early as mid-1942, but he was later killed, being shot down by *Flak* during a low level attack on a Sicilian airfield.

Sandy Johnstone spent time on Eisenhower's staff before going out to serve with the RAF Delegation in Washington, whilst Gerry Edge commanded the 84 Group Control Centre with 2nd TAF and received an OBE.

Others who became Station Commanders or were involved in training at this rank included William Clyde, George Denholm, Andrew Farquhar and Sir Adrian Hope.

A further seven, at least, became wing commanders. Tony Eyre and Joe Kayll both led Spitfire Wings from England, but both were shot down over France, becoming POWs. Bill Douglas was also a Wing Leader in the UK later in the war, while Paul Webb undertook a similar role in Italy with the Balkan Air Force. William Blackadder commanded the Air Fighting Development Unit at Wittering for a time, and Andy McDowell was commanding officer of No 616 Sqn in 1944 when it became the RAF's first jet fighter unit.

In summary, therefore, what did the Auxiliary Air Force achieve? Clearly it formed a valuable resource for Fighter Command particularly, given the circumstances, during 1940. It provided a number of notable leaders for the later years of the war, and it also provided a group of named squadrons with which the inhabitants of the related cities and counties throughout the UK could identify and consider 'their own'.

However, I believe that I have demonstrated that the publicity which the AAF has received, and the claims made to 'own' the performance and service of squadrons carrying the old AAF numbers, long after they had ceased to be 'auxiliary' units in anything other than name, have somewhat overstated its true achievements.

In particular, the impression that the AAF units which fought in the Battle of Britain were predominantly manned by the 'weekend warriors' not only considerably exaggerates the case, but fails to give due credit to the more numerous, and equally successful, regulars and VRs who, in practice, made up the greater part of the establishment of most of these squadrons for much of the latter half of 1940.

On the debit side, the activities and recruiting policies of some of these units during the 1930s led many to gain the impression that the members of these squadrons were arrogant and snobbish, considering themselves to be a privileged élite – an impression which appears on occasion not to have been undeserved. Had these young men, with their sports cars, hunters and Saville Row uniforms, with the tunics lined in red silk, been a little more liberal in their entry policies, the RAF might have had rather more trained pilots in the AAF and fewer vacant slots to fill from the slim reserves of the regular RAF.

Why did they receive such good publicity, raising the perception of their contributions so high? Looking at the contacts many of these pilots undoubtedly had, given the social circles in which they moved, they seem to have had many friends in high places, ready and willing to speak well of them. Indeed, some reached positions of considerable influence in their later careers.

To say the least, for that most 'auxiliary' of AAF units, No 601 Sqn (known at times as the 'Millionaires' Squadron'), to have included within its ranks Max Aitken, son of Lord Beaverbrook, and heir to the Beaverbrook Press empire, cannot have done them any harm. No more can the appointment of Sir Hugh Dundas, late of No 616 Sqn, and a dedicated auxiliary, as Chairman of Independent Television.

Nonetheless, given the ethos of the day, the squadrons possessed the great advantage of being there when they were needed most, their pilots performing with unquestioned gallantry, devotion and a remarkable degree of skill. On balance my own view is that the positives greatly outweigh the negatives, so no demolition job here! In the modern parlance, 'The Boys Done Good!'

Note. *As he explained at the time, because the programme was already running late, Chris Shores elected to omit his summary of the later wartime activities of the nominally AAF squadrons and his highlighting of the careers of selected prominent AAF pilots. Most of the text appearing on pages 54-61 was not, therefore, actually delivered on the day, but it is reproduced here for completeness. This omission also gave rise to some of the points raised from the floor in the subsequent discussion; these points have nevertheless also been recorded. While adding this footnote, I will take the opportunity to sponsor my own candidate for an AAF 'Oscar', my nominee being Wg Cdr James Bazin who was credited with ten victories while flying with No 607 Sqn in 1940 before demonstrating a remarkable degree of adaptability by switching to Lancasters, flying twenty-five sorties as OC No 9 Sqn.* **Ed**

MORNING DISCUSSION PERIOD

John Davis. Could you tell us a little bit more about the 11.5 million-strong pre-war vote for peace? I was alive then, but I don't remember it!

Dr Mansell. It was Canon Dick Shepherd who started the ball rolling by asking people to sign, what he called, the Peace Pledge. The response was so encouraging that it led him to establish the Peace Pledge Union. In 1935 this organisation conducted a house-to-house ballot which involved people knocking on doors and asking folk to sign a pro-forma indicating that they supported the idea of all international problems being solved by peaceful means, with the League of Nations being promoted as the appropriate forum for settling such disputes, much as the UN is supposed to do today. The fact that this initiative succeeded in attracting some 11.5 million signatures was clearly something that the Air Ministry needed to take into account. After all, it appeared that a very substantial proportion of the population was saying that it did not wish to be associated with military solutions, which must have given the government food for thought, as it was just about to embark on a massive rearmament programme.

Bill Beaumont. I think that it is worth reminding ourselves that we are today removed from the Falklands War by about the same twenty-year interval as that which separated the people who signed the Peace Pledge from the horrors of 1914-18. We all remember the Falklands; how much more vividly must they have remembered the Great War? I think that the comparison is an interesting one and one which makes it easier to understand the attitudes of the 'appeasers' of the 1930s.

AVM Newton. A good point. Thank you. It is quite easy to forget that the Royal Air Force was itself only 21 years old when WW II began.

Sir Hector Monro. I felt that all three presentations were very interesting, although there was, I think, just a suspicion of criticism of the auxiliaries, both pre-war and even in the Battle of Britain. I do think that that is quite unjustified. I am sure that the statistics which we were shown are accurate, but the only fact that really matters is that we could not conceivably have won the Battle of Britain without the Auxiliary Air Force. Surely that is what we should be focusing on and not individual statistics comparing VRs, regulars and auxiliaries. It was the 'squadrons' that were doing the work and it was squadron spirit that permitted them to achieve so much.

Prof Kenneth Short. I was interested to hear mention of Lord Rothermere's brainchild, the National League of Airmen, as it appears to have made a very important contribution to forcing along the development of the Volunteer Reserve. The League supported rearmament during the 1935 election and then put forward a plan for the training of pilots for the RAF. If you study, for instance, the correspondence between Lord Swinton, at the Air Ministry, and the Treasury, you can see that the Government was under a great deal of pressure to adopt the Rothermere Plan. There were suggestions that the Ministry was dragging its feet and that delay could have major political consequences. I wonder if you have anything further to add regarding the influence of the National League of Airmen's plans on hastening the announcement of the establishment of the VR in the summer of 1936.

Mansell. The National League of Airmen, the NLA, and the ALBE, the Air League of the British Empire, were both interested in exploiting the flying club movement. In 1936 the National League approached the Air Ministry with a plan for, what they called, Business Houses Flying Clubs. The notion was that fifty business houses would each sponsor a flying club and that the men joining these clubs would be available for service in the event of an emergency. Coincidentally, this proposal was submitted to the Ministry just as it was considering the creation of the VR.

Swinton was rather thrown by this idea because it would clearly compete with the Volunteer Reserve concept because most of the candidates who elected to join one of the Business Houses Flying Clubs would have represented a lost recruit for the VR. That having been said, I am sure that you are right to suggest that the kind of external pressure that was being exerted by organisations like the NLA and the ALBE was encouraging to the Air Ministry. It was certainly symptomatic of a ground swell of opinion that indicated that there was positive support for a substantial increase in reserve forces.

As Tedder immediately recognised, however, there was a problem with using flying clubs. A club-based movement would plainly be run on *civilian* lines and Tedder wanted a *Royal Air Force* Volunteer Reserve in which the commitment to serve was to be an integral and essential element of the ethos. Similarly, Chamier's advocacy of his Citizens Air Force, which was very closely allied to the NLA proposals, has to be seen in the context of Tedder's demand for a strictly *military* reserve.

Nevertheless, while the NLA's concept could not satisfy the Ministry's requirements entirely, I am sure that it made a positive contribution to finding solutions to the problems involved in devising a means of increasing the number of available pilots through some kind of direct appeal to the public, rather than by expanding the regular air force.

In this context, I think that I have to mention the AAF again. It simply did not represent a solution to the problem. Gaining entry to the AAF was not easy, the contemporary documentation is quite clear on this, which meant that, no matter how good it was, it was not a suitable means for creating a reserve on the scale required. Given the nature of its organisation and its culture, there was no way that the AAF could have coped with 5000 volunteer reservist pilots drawn from a wide social spectrum. That is not to decry the AAF, but it is a fact.

Short. Thank you. I think that it is worth pointing out, just for the record, that the flying clubs which actually existed, as distinct from those which might have been created in response to Rothermere's scheme, were underwritten by the Air Ministry. It is also worth pointing out that the Ministry often notes that it did not think that it was getting its money's worth.

Sir John Barraclough. I was very impressed, as I am sure that we all were, by the league table comparison of the performance of the auxiliary fighter squadrons *vis-à-vis* the regular units, and with the fact that they featured so strongly at the top of the table up to and including the Battle of Britain. With the Battle of the Atlantic approaching its designated 60th Anniversary next year, could I suggest that this meeting should also take a sideways glance at the performance of the other auxiliary squadrons, those which did not serve in the fighter role but which flew on maritime patrol and anti-submarine duties. I suspect that we might find that their comparative performance was equally favourable. I have in mind No 500 (County of Kent) Sqn, in particular, which, after initial service in the UK with Ansons, re-equipped with Hudsons which it took to North Africa where it was outstandingly successful in its attacks on Italian and German submarines. I do not have any figures to hand but I hope that I am right in thinking that its record would have come pretty near to those of the famous Nos 120 and 269 Sqns which operated over the mid-Atlantic from Iceland.

If the legend is correct, I think that No 500 Sqn could also claim a place in the fighter squadron table, because, while operating from Detling in the early days of WW II, its Ansons managed to shoot down two Messerschmitt 109s, probably using a local modification sponsored by the auxiliaries which involved increasing the armament by installing additional beam guns using mountings knocked up by the local village blacksmith.

My point is, that, if the analysis could be extended, I am sure that it would show that the spirit, verve and determination of the auxiliary squadrons meant that they all did very well by comparison with the regulars in the league tables.

Jefford. If I could just make a comment. I think that it is important to recognise, and this is a point that Chris made, that as the war went on the auxiliary squadrons became less and less 'auxiliary'. It is true that their number plates were sustained but the constitution of the manpower involved changed quite rapidly. By 1941 most of the original AAF aircrew had moved on or become casualties. It is also worth pointing out that the only aircrew involved would have been pilots; there were very few (if any) AAF observers and there would have been no auxiliaries at all among the later aircrew categories, navigators, air bombers, flight engineers and the like.

Many of the surviving auxiliary pilots were still flying in 1941 and later, of course, but the point is that very few of them were still serving with the auxiliary squadrons. Similarly, the groundcrew element was subject to a continual process of dilution and we must bear in mind that on the outbreak of war (balloon units aside) the overall manning level with respect to AAF groundcrew had stood at only 66%. This figure could never be improved upon, of course, because recruiting immediately ceased. The squadrons were rapidly brought up to full establishment by posting in regulars and ever increasing numbers of VR airmen. Establishments also tended to expand during the early years of the war, these increases drawing in yet more non-AAF bodies while those auxiliary airmen who became officers were discharged from the AAF and commissioned into the RAFVR. All of these factors contributed to a steady dilution of the 'auxiliary' nature of a nominally auxiliary squadron. Thus, while I would not dispute No 500 Sqn's admirable operational record in 1942 and later, one has to ask just how much of this achievement was attributable to AAF personnel.

This rather loops back to Lord Monro's earlier observation. It is not the intention of any of today's speakers to be critical. Today is not about iconoclasm, but it is about objectivity. What we have been trying to establish is the extent to which 'auxiliariness' was a factor during WW II. What the statistics showed is that the auxiliaries were still an identifiable group with a tangible presence up to and including the Battle of Britain, although even then they were perhaps not quite as numerous as we might have imagined. Thereafter, they rapidly melted away and were soon absorbed into, and became virtually indistinguishable from, all of the other personnel, and units, within the vastly expanded society of the wartime air force.

After Note. Sir John Barraclough was curious to know what sort of showing was made by the four squadrons which bore AAF number plates while operating in the maritime role. It was apparent from other comments made on the day that there were some reservations about using statistics but they really are rather difficult to avoid and they do present a practical means of measuring, at least *prima facie*, comparative performance. The figures that follow (Source: Norman Franks' *Search, Find and Kill*; Grub Street, 1995) reflect the 'top half' of the league table of wartime anti-submarine squadrons; it does not include maritime strike units, although Beaufighters and Mosquitos (and even Typhoons) did account for a number of U-Boats. Plainly, all four 'auxiliary' units were comfortably in the top half of the table, with No 502 Sqn probably doing the greatest amount of damage.

Expanding on Sir John's reference to No 500 Sqn's early success in air combat, its performance was actually even more remarkable than he suggested. By the close of the Battle of Britain period the squadron claimed to have destroyed three Bf 109s, a Bf 110 and a He 111, and to have probably destroyed or damaged at least five other enemy aircraft, including a pair of Hs 126s. Not bad going for Ansons.

Unit	Sunk	Sunk (shared)	Damaged	Damaged (shared)	Total
120 Sqn	12	3	9		24
224 Sqn	10	1	7	3	21
86 Sqn	13	1	4		18
172 Sqn	8	1	8	1	18
179 Sqn	11		1	2	14
206 Sqn	7	2	4		13
202 Sqn	6	1	5	1	13
58 Sqn	5	2	3		10
10 Sqn RAAF	5	1	4		10
210 Sqn	5		5		10
233 Sqn	5	1	2	2	10
502 Sqn	**2**	**2**	**5**	**1**	**10**
228 Sqn	4	2	3		9
269 Sqn	5		3		8
53 Sqn	4		3	1	8
59 Sqn	3	2	3		8
461 Sqn RAAF	5	1		1	7
220 Sqn	5		2		7
500 Sqn	**4**	**2**	**1**		**7**
201 Sqn	5		1		6
162 Sqn RCAF	5		1		6
407 Sqn RCAF	4		1	1	6
612 Sqn	**2**	**1**	**1**	**2**	**6**
423 Sqn RCAF	3		2		5
311 (Czech) Sqn	2	2	1		5
48 Sqn	2	1	1	1	5
10 OTU	2		3		5
304 (Polish) Sqn	2		2		4
608 Sqn	**1**	**1**	**2**		**4**
230 Sqn	3				3
200 Sqn	2				2
221 Sqn	2				2
36 Sqn	1	1			2
547 Sqn	1		1		2
330 (Norwegian) Sqn	1		1		2
333 (Norwegian) Sqn	1		1		2

Submarines sunk or damaged by units operating under RAF control.

UNIVERSITY AIR SQUADRONS IN WW II

Wing Commander Gerry Margiotta

Wg Cdr Gerry Margiotta, had an unbroken run of 26 years in flying appointments, some of it on Vulcans; much of it at Cranwell, where he served variously as a QFI, OC 1 Sqn, OC Standards and Deputy CFI. There is another common thread running through this pattern as Gerry has also had repeated links with the University Air Squadrons. Indeed he began his flying career in 1959 with Manchester UAS and subsequently commanded the Oxford UAS. Now nominally retired, he is currently the Ground Training Officer at HQ Elementary Flying Training, which puts him back at Cranwell, yet again, and sustains his link to the UASs.

There is a certain lack of awareness about the history of the UASs, especially about their function and status during the Second World War. I was, therefore, specifically asked to concentrate on *that* period during my presentation. I will, nevertheless, start with a little pre-history and wind-up with a brief current SITREP.

Trenchard had always envisaged that his peacetime air force would draw heavily on the universities; indeed, he made four references to them in his 1919 Memorandum. At the time, he did not go so far as specifically to advocate establishing a presence on campus, but this idea soon crystallised and UASs were set up at Cambridge and Oxford in 1925. At this stage the aim of the game was to promote 'air mindedness' and to stimulate an interest in, and research into, matters aeronautical. Although the UASs were staffed and funded by the Air Ministry, membership involved no Service obligations whatsoever; members were not subject to the Air Force Act and they did not wear uniform. Indeed, practical flying was not addressed very seriously until 1928.

By 1931 the procedures had become sufficiently well defined to permit them to be turned into a set of formal regulations via the publication of the first edition of AP1401. The new AP restricted membership to seventy-five per squadron, based on annual intakes of twenty-five for three-year courses. It also specified the content of the Proficiency Certificate. This required attendance at an annual camp, the

Bristol Fighter, F4542, of Cambridge UAS in 1931.

accumulation of at least fifteen flying hours (three of them solo) and passing examinations in the theory of flight, rigging, engines, airmanship and air pilotage – what we could call navigation. As stated in AP1401, the aims of the UASs were now 'to encourage an interest in flying', as well as promoting research into technical matters *and* to 'assist those who might wish to join the RAF'.

Clearly, therefore, while it was still quite low-key, at least the *idea* of, recruiting had been tacked onto the agenda by 1931 and from 1937 onwards UAS members were being actively encouraged to join the RAF, the RAFO or the RAFVR, when they went down and a substantial proportion of them did just that. By this time there was a third UAS, London having opened one in 1935, and the standard trainer had become the Avro Tutor.

The next significant event occurred in May 1939 when the Military Training Act introduced an obligation for young men aged 20-21, including undergraduates, to register for military service. This involved a liability to be called up for a six-month stint of full-time training (although, in the event, this option was not actually exercised). Anyone who had signed on as a reservist *prior* to April, however, was exempt the period of military training and some judicious rule-bending resulted in forty-four members of the Oxford UAS, thirty-six at Cambridge and, presumably, a similar number at London, being hastily inducted into the RAFVR in arrears. This gave the UASs a slightly more military air but it

Cambridge UAS again, this time a Tutor.

was all a bit academic as all three squadrons were disbanded following the declaration of war in September 1939.

A year later, in August 1940 the Air Ministry became aware that the War Office had stolen a march on them by gaining Treasury approval for a scheme whereby the Army would sponsor young men for a six-month stint at university followed by the granting of a commission in the RA, the RE or the Royal Signals. Caught on the back foot, the Air Ministry promptly set about devising a parallel scheme to ensure that the RAF got its fair share of this high grade material.

Early ideas envisaged the completion of the elementary phase of formal flying training while at university but these were soon abandoned in favour of a one-year course of academic study during which, via membership of a re-established UAS, the candidate would also undergo military training equivalent to that provided by the (then) ten-week course at an Initial Training Wing – an ITW. On successfully clearing all the hurdles, he would be enlisted into the RAFVR and proceed directly to flying training, that is to say, by-passing the ITW course. All other things being equal, on gaining his flying badge he would be commissioned.

This is more or less what happened, except that the so-called 'University Course for Candidates for Aircrew Duties' turned out to be of only six month's duration, rather than twelve. Once the UASs had been re-established, membership was not confined exclusively to Short Course students and ordinary undergraduates were also encouraged to join. Indeed, since it was evident that the universities held substantial numbers of young men who wished to join the RAF it had been decided to establish a UAS wherever it could be justified by the local demand, irrespective of whether or not the university was participating in the Short Course scheme. Furthermore, while the stated aim of the wartime UASs was primarily to do with recruiting aircrew and/or providing them with pre-entry training, space was also found for undergraduate entrants who wished to join the Technical or A&SD Branches.

The Oxford and Cambridge squadrons were re-opened in October 1940 with others being established during 1941. In the context of today's seminar, it is probably worth observing that much of the spadework involved in this project was done by a prominent pre-war Auxiliary Air Force officer, Wg Cdr Lord Nigel Douglas-Hamilton who was instrumental in ensuring that there were eventually as many as twenty-three wartime UASs, as listed at Figure 1.

I will stress once again, just to make it absolutely clear, that the primary purpose of the wartime UASs was to provide *pre-entry* training for potential *aircrew* officers. What they specifically did *not* do, however, was to provide any form of *flying* training. Most units did 'own' a solitary Tiger Moth, even the odd Oxford, but these were for the benefit of the staff, not the students. That is not to say that the occasional air experience flights were not laid on but most of these would have been in Ansons or the like.

Apart from a general soaking in the university atmosphere, all Short Course students were required to attend a specifically designed series of lectures covering mathematics and mechanics plus a secondary subject chosen from electricity and magnetism, engineering, meteorology or navigation. In practice, a university's ability to offer secondary subjects depended upon the capacity of its academic staff and a student's 'choice' could be limited, at Manchester, Edinburgh and Aberdeen, for instance, to Met. Beyond that, the aim of the game was to obtain a UAS Proficiency Certificate. This now covered mathematics, navigation, drill, physical training, signals, anti-gas procedures, armament, air force law, discipline, admin and org, hygiene, sanitation, aircraft recognition, general studies and the Link Trainer. In other words, the subjects covered by the ITW syllabus.

UNIVERSITY	FORMED	DISBANDED
Cambridge	October 1940	–*
Oxford	October 1940	–*
Leeds	January 1941	–
Liverpool	January 1941	–
Edinburgh	January 1941	–*
Glasgow	January 1941	–
Aberdeen	January 1941	–
Belfast	January 1941	–*
St Andrews	January 1941	–*
Aberystwyth	January 1941	–
Durham	February 1941	–*
Manchester	February 1941	–
Southampton	February 1941	–*
Swansea	February 1941	–
Bristol	February 1941	–
Cardiff	March 1941	October 1943
Sheffield	March 1941	October 1943
Hull	March 1941	October 1943
Reading	March 1941	October 1943
London	April 1941	–
Birmingham	May 1941	–
Nottingham	May 1941	–
Exeter	August 1941	October 1943

* Still offering a Short Course in January 1944.

Fig 1. *University Air Squadrons formed during WW II.*

So far, so good, but where did the UASs fit within the RAF's wartime organisational 'wiring diagram'? It will, I suspect, come as something of a surprise to many of you to learn that they were part of the Air Training Corps. Indeed, while UAS members wore the uniform of RAF airmen, these were embellished with ATC buttons and cap badges, *not* those of the RAF. This came about as a result of a major reappraisal of all aspects of pre-entry training in late 1940. The rash of UASs which was about to be established was clearly going to be a part of the overall pre-entry picture and it was necessary to find a convenient means of plugging them into the chain of command. Since the Air Training Corps was also being set up at the same time it was decided to integrate the UASs within that organisation. The ATC was formally established by a Royal Warrant of 4 February 1941 which left no doubt as to the constitutional position of the wartime UASs. It stated that 'there shall be established a Corps to be called the Air Training Corps' and that the Corps 'shall comprise squadrons formed at universities and university colleges to be known as university air squadrons.'

To begin with the UASs were subordinated to HQ 54 Gp but in January 1942 the Air Ministry assumed direct responsibility for administration, as well as policy, although for mundane day-to-day matters, each squadron was affiliated to a nearby RAF unit.

The size of the establishment varied widely from squadron to squadron. In April 1942, for instance, eleven UASs were commanded by wing commanders, three by squadron leaders and the rest by flight lieutenants. At that stage, Cambridge, the largest, had a staff of thirteen, six officers, four NCOs and three civilians, while, at the other extreme, Cardiff had just three, a flight lieutenant, a flight sergeant and a single civilian.

The first Short Course began in April 1941 and ended in September. Of the intake of 278, 270 (or 97%) were recommended for commissions. That compares to only 322 (or 57%) of the 563 undergraduate members of the UASs who had volunteered for aircrew duties.

A head count of *undergraduate* entrants as at 1 April 1942 shows that the total membership of the twenty-three UASs stood at 1085 potential aircrew plus 168 technical officers, one administrator and seventy-four Fleet Air Arm candidates, the RAF being content to make room for these dark blue cuckoos in its light blue nest throughout the war. As with the staff, however, the distribution of this population varied widely. There were, for instance, 178 at Cambridge, eighty-nine at Manchester and only twenty-one at Exeter. But these were *undergrads*; what of the Short Course entrants, which was what it was really all about?

Ten universities were involved in the early stages but three of them, Glasgow, Manchester and Aberdeen, were on a relatively small scale and they dropped out in 1942. Figure 2 shows the overall intake into the nine wartime courses. This was, incidentally, well below the notional capacity as financial approval had been given for up to 2000 per year so the total of 5639 shown here could have been as many 9000.

Cse No	Intake		Participating UASs
	Date	**Number**	
1	Apr 41	278	Oxford, Cambridge, Durham, St Andrews, Edinburgh, Glasgow, Manchester, Aberdeen (8)
2	Oct 41	500	Oxford, Cambridge, Durham, St Andrews, Edinburgh, Glasgow, Manchester, Aberdeen, Belfast, Southampton (10)
3	Apr 42	544	"
4	Oct 42	862	Oxford, Cambridge, Durham, St Andrews, Edinburgh, Belfast, Southampton (7)
5	Apr 43	817	"
6	Oct 43	993	"
7	Apr 44	614	"
8	Oct 44	881	"
9	Apr 45	150	Oxford, Cambridge, Durham, St Andrews, Southampton (5)
	Total	5639	

Fig 2. Wartime UAS Short Course Intakes.

UAS	Intake	Failed	Suspended	Output	Success
Oxford	192	10	2	180	93.8%
Cambridge	309	6	12	291	94.2%
Durham	107	8	6	93	86.9%
Edinburgh	25	0	1	24	96.0%
Belfast	54	3	4	47	87.0%
St Andrews	95	0	0	95	100.0%
Southampton	80	0	0	80	100.0%
Totals	862	27	25	810	**94.0%**

Fig 3. Performance of 4th UAS Short Course Intake (Oct 42-Apr 43)

UAS	Aircrew	Other	Total
Oxford	6	0	6
Cambridge	18	6	24
Durham	16	2	18
Edinburgh	8	0	8
Belfast	15	1	16
St Andrews	8	0	8
Southampton	4	1	5
London	118	35	153
Glasgow	19	1	20
Manchester	15	8	23
Leeds	59	6	65
Aberdeen	9	0	9
Liverpool	7	0	7
Aberystwyth	9	2	11
Bristol	35	1	36
Swansea	28	16	44
Birmingham	15	12	27
Nottingham	46	7	53
Totals	**435**	**98**	**533**

Fig 4. Undergraduate UAS membership in Jan 44.

Figure 3 shows the performance of the fourth cohort, a typical mid-war intake. As you can see, at 94% the overall success rate was remarkably high. Specific figures do not appear to have survived but there are references on file to performance 'improving' so, if we just take the 94% figure shown here and apply it to the total intake of 5639 it would seem that at least 5300 will have benefited from the Short Course.

In 1943 a concession which had permitted 18-year olds to defer their military service in order to attend a one-year Arts course was withdrawn. This significantly reduced the undergraduate recruiting pool as a result of which five of the weaker squadrons were closed down: Hull, Cardiff, Reading, Exeter and Sheffield.

In January 1944 overall undergraduate membership of the remaining eighteen UASs stood at 533 (less than half of what it had been two years before) plus almost 1000 Short Course students at the seven universities which were still participating in that scheme – the first seven in Figure 4. The uneven distribution of the undergraduate membership was becoming increasingly marked, 50% of the 533 being concentrated at London, Leeds and Swansea while six squadrons now had fewer than ten undergraduate members each.

By mid-1944 the aircrew shortage of 1940-41 had been converted into a surplus such that the output of the October Short Course would have to wait at least six months before they could be fed into flying training. In view of the improving war situation, there was little likelihood of anyone on later courses ever becoming operational so admission to the April 1945 intake was limited to just 150 (see Figure 2), all of whom would be required to sign an undertaking that they would be prepared to serve in a *peacetime* air force. This was seen, in part, to be an interim measure to tide the RAF over until the pre-war Cranwell cadetship scheme, and more conventional university recruiting mechanisms, could be reinstated. Because of the reduced numbers, Edinburgh and Belfast were deleted from the Short Course scheme leaving only five participating squadrons.

The next, the tenth, and as it turned out, last 'Short' Course began in October 1945 and was actually of one (academic) year's duration. The RAF had not particularly wanted a longer course but, as in 1940, it had been wrong-footed by the Army which had gained financial approval for a year-long course so we had to have one too, the stated rationale simply being that 'the Air Ministry cannot reasonably be asked to lag behind the War Office in this matter.' Hardly the most considered of justifications for spending public money.

The period embracing the ending of the war was one of considerable uncertainty, of course, because there were so many unanswered questions to frustrate the planners. Of particular significance in the context of the UASs were the following. Would they be retained at all and, if so, in what form and for what purpose? Would conscription be sustained? How big would the post-war air force be? These nettles were first grasped in February 1945 at the 11th Meeting of the Post-War Reserves Committee whose recommendations included:

a. The retention of UASs at Oxford, Cambridge, London and at least seven of the larger provincial universities.

b. The decoupling of UASs from the ATC and the absorption of their members into the RAFVR.

c. The minimum size of a UAS should be twenty-five members.

d. Flying training should be reinstated.

e. All COs should be regular officers (not RAFVR or RAFO, as had often been the case during the war) and university staff serving as instructors should do so as civilians.

f. The training commitment should involve: 110 hours of ground instruction per year; half-a-day per week of flying during term and attendance at a fourteen-day annual camp.

Much of this had congealed into policy by March 1946 when DGT, AVM Sir Basil Embry, chaired a meeting, attended by representatives from eight universities. This more or less endorsed the RAF's proposals with some necessary amplification and clarification. For instance: members were to be enlisted in the RAFVR as airmen but with officer cadet status; the ground training commitment was to be significantly reduced and the flying training content was set at 20 hours per year. Priority was to be given to ex-schoolboys but there were unlikely to be many of these to begin with because 90% of the 1946 university intake had been reserved for ex-Servicemen. So long as it did not work to the detriment of the school candidates, it was also agreed that qualified wartime pilots who had returned to university to complete their studies and who had elected to join the RAFVR, would be permitted to 'keep their hands in' via membership of the UAS.

The long and short of all this was that in the autumn of 1946 the UASs resumed something like their pre-war activities, except that there were now fourteen of them, rather than just three, and they were flying Tiger Moths rather than Tutors.[1]

In June 1947 a new Royal Warrant governing the ATC was issued. This mentioned only those UASs which were *not* 'squadrons of Our Air Force Volunteer Reserve'. There were only three of these, Durham, Leeds and St Andrews, and steps were immediately taken to have their members enrolled within the RAFVR, thus severing the final ties with the ATC.

---

[1]Although it took until the autumn of 1946 to set up the overall post-war UAS organisation, the better-established, ie older/larger, squadrons had already reintroduced flying training, albeit on a limited scale. Cambridge, for instance, was operating three Tiger Moths by the spring of 1946, the first post-war undergraduate to go solo probably being M T Moore of Pembroke College on 18th January.

Tiger Moth, EM816, of Nottingham UAS in 1947.

By November of 1947 the post-war arrangements were sufficiently routine to permit the drafting of a new edition of AP1401. It is worth comparing the introduction to this edition with that of its pre-war predecessors. In January 1931 (and again in January 1935) AP 1401 had stated that: 'The object of the University Air Squadrons generally is to encourage an interest in flying and to promote and maintain a liaison with the Universities in technical and research problems affecting aviation.' The 1947 edition said that the 'purpose of University Air Squadrons is to provide training during their university career for members of the universities who wish to prepare themselves for commissioned service in the General Duties branch and the Technical branch of the regular or non-regular air forces...' Clearly, there had been a major shift in emphasis. Before the war the UASs had been about 'air mindedness'. Now they were about officer recruiting.

Incidentally, the 1947 edition of AP1401 also made it quite clear, in para 1, that the UAS's 'form part of the RAFVR', thus justifying their inclusion in today's programme. Having reached 1947, I can also reasonably claim to have satisfied my brief so I will conclude with a short update.

Although the UASs were up and running again there was still a lingering ambivalence about their purpose. Were they really about recruiting, about flying training, or were they simply an investment in the future by ensuring that tomorrow's great and good would look favourably upon the RAF after their exposure to it via their UAS experience? As a result, the post-war era has been punctuated by a series of reviews each

A sign of the times – a civil-registered Grob Tutor, G-BYVI, of East Lowlands UAS in 2000.

of which examined the rationale behind, and the depth of the RAF's commitment to, the UAS concept. Each one concluded that the movement *did* earn its keep, although there were occasional cut backs resulting in squadrons being closed, not to mention the odd shotgun marriage.

Meanwhile the aeroplanes in use evolved from Tiger Moths through Chipmunks, via the occasional Harvard, to Bulldogs. In a rationalisation of resources in the mid-1990s each of the Air Experience Flights, whose role is to fly ATC cadets, was merged with a UAS, producing faint echoes of WW II. Ten years before this, in 1985, another milestone had been passed when the first women were admitted to UASs as pilots.

Today we have fifteen squadrons and the standard training aeroplane is the Grob Tutor. As in the past, membership is open to officers of ground branches but the aim of the game is to ensure a flow of pilots. Students fall into three categories, those attending university on RAF cadetships, those on RAF bursaries and those who are recruited on campus. As in 1947, all are still enlisted into the RAFVR, technically as airmen, but with the status of officer cadets, with a heavy emphasis being placed on the 'officer' aspect. In the bizarre 'accountant speak' to which the air force is increasingly prone, we are deemed to be 'cost neutral' if we can secure an inflow of eighty pilots per year. This we do. In fact some 60% of the RAF's pilots now join via the UASs and if we were to close them down today it is difficult to see how we could sustain our pilot training system.

POST-WAR RAF RESERVES TO 1960

Wing Commander 'Jeff' Jefford

Due to the inevitable uncertainties that abounded in 1945, the Post-War Reserves Committee had to deal with some grey areas when it was trying to nail down the initial arrangements for a reconstituted Volunteer Reserve. Would conscription continue in peacetime, for instance, and just how large a reserve was going to be required (could be afforded)?

Without definitive answers to such questions, a lot of assumptions had to be made and one of these was that the RAFVR would be reinstated on broadly similar lines to those that had existed before the war. This implied a need for units similar to the civilian-managed pre-war ERFTSs to provide both refresher and *ab initio* flying training. Compared to the air force of the 1930s, however, the post-war RAF had matured into a far more complex organisation which fully recognised the need for professional aircrew other than pilots.

Unfortunately, many of these back-seaters required training facilities at least *as* sophisticated, and often *more* sophisticated, than those needed by pilots. While a Tiger Moth might suffice to permit a pilot to recharge his batteries by slipping 'the surly bonds of earth', it would be of little use to a navigator or a signaller – and a Moth offered even less prospect of job satisfaction to an air engineer or a gunner.

By September 1946 the numbers had begun to crystallise, the Defence Committee having decided to authorise an active air force reserve of 72 000. With 12 000 of these earmarked for the AAF, it was assumed that one third of the remainder would be VR flying personnel, leaving 40 000 as groundcrew. The representation of aircrew categories among the 20 000 VR aviators was to reflect the crew compositions of the current 134-squadron regular air force, which meant that there were to be 7300 pilots, 4800 navigators, 3600 signallers, 2000 engineers and 2300 gunners.

To begin with there would be no *ab initio* flying because it was anticipated that all 20 000 aircrew would be wartime veterans. It was intended to provide the pilots and navs with 20 hours' flying during a concentrated fifteen-day annual training session plus a further 20 hours spread across the year. Signallers were to gain their airborne experience on the backs of the navigators; engineers and gunners were to be trained on the ground at Town Centres.

Once the numbers had been crunched, it was calculated that the scheme would require no fewer than 600 Tiger Moths and 160 Ansons. This plan was approved and authority was given for the formation of twenty-five Reserve Flying Schools (RFS). Each RFS was to have two flights, each of a dozen Tiger Moths plus a flight of six or seven navigation trainers.

Meanwhile, matters of this nature had become the province of the Auxiliary and Reserve Forces Committee which met for the first time in December 1946. Because there was some vagueness over the rationale underlying the original distribution of aircrew categories, one of the committee's first actions was to seek clarification of the composition of the 20 000 VR aircrew. The Stats staff chewed the figures over and in February 1947 they came up with a set of revised figures. There were now to be 9320 pilots, 4740 navs, 2860 signallers, 1120 engineers and 1960 gunners.

It got more complicated, however, because the committee took a further step back and queried the basic breakdown of the entire 72 000. It will be recalled that it had initially been assumed that the AAF would need 12 000. Since then, it had been agreed that, apart from its twenty flying squadrons, the AAF would also have twenty Regiment squadrons and numerous Air Defence Units. The overall manpower bill for this lot was now estimated to be 26 400. Because the total of 72 000 was sacrosanct, and 20 000 of them were to be VR aircrew, the VR groundcrew component dropped to a mere 25 600.

Despite these wobbles, in April 1947 His Majesty approved a revised set of regulations for the RAFVR to cover the post-war case. There were to be four types of membership:

1. Ex-Servicemen who had *not* been regulars (Class E and the RAFO catered for ex-regulars who had a reserve obligation).
2. Direct entrants, preferably with an appropriate qualification or experience.
3. ATC and CCF officers.
4. UAS students.

At the same time, 'VR' badges (small gilt monograms to be worn on the uniform collar for officers and cloth patches to be worn on the upper sleeve for airmen) were reinstated, and the very similar 'VRT' emblems for ATC and CCF officers were introduced. Conceived before the war as a mark of distinction, to differentiate between *volunteer* reservists and the

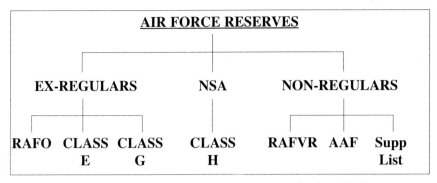

Fig 1. Schematic of reserve structure in the late 1940s.

ex-regulars who had a reserve *obligation*, the 'VR' emblems were not actually introduced until September 1939 after which all new entrants wore them, regardless of whether they were volunteers or conscripts. In effect, the 'VR' tag now served only to mark the wartime 'amateur' from the pre-war regular 'professional'. As such it became a divisive influence and by June 1943 AMP had concluded that 'the VR badge has actually been harmful and may become so to an increasing degree.' All RAFVR officers were, therefore, instructed to cease wearing the badge, leaving them with neat holes in the collars of their tunics. Since many airmen had already stopped wearing their 'VR' patches, no formal prohibition was issued in their case and they were simply allowed to fade away.[1]

So, armed with a new edition of AP938 and with its badges restored, the peacetime VR was back in business, recruiting (initially only for pilots) having begun on 15 March. The field was subsequently extended to include navs and signallers in February 1948, officers in selected ground trades from May and ground tradesmen from October.

Before considering the subsequent evolution of the RAFVR, this is as convenient a place as any to insert a wiring diagram of the overall structure of the early post-war reserves (see Figure 1).

On the left we have released personnel, all of whom could be recalled to the colours in an emergency but most of whom had little or no training commitment. The RAFO – the Reserve of Air Force Officers – was much

---

[1] A corresponding prohibition was not placed on the very similar auxiliary 'A' because there were relatively few of them left by mid-1943 and it was considered that this emblem did still exert a positive influence.

the same as it had been before the war; it consisted of ex-regular officers *with* a reserve obligation but it is worth noting that it was restyled the RAFRO – the Royal Air Force Reserve of Officers – in 1950.

Class E reservists were ex-regular airmen *with* a reserve obligation and, because there had not yet been time for any post-war entrants to complete their engagements, they were mostly pre-war old-timers who had been called up in 1939 and had since been put out to grass again; by 1948 there were only about 650 of them still on the books.

Class G had been set up in 1945 to handle airmen on 'emergency engagements'. In essence, that meant wartime RAFVR men and post-war National Servicemen, because conscription under 1939 rules was still in force. In 1948 there were about 800 000 Class G reservists and they were all subject to recall for 'the duration of the present emergency'; that was the 1939 emergency, and it too was still in force.

Class H was a new invention to cater specifically for men conscripted under the revised terms of the 1948 National Service Act (NSA) so it would be 1950 before it took on a tangible form. Class H reservists were *liable* to be recalled for training but this option was not exercised to any significant degree, most being left in peace once they had completed the full-time portion of their engagement. This rather laid-back RAF approach would, incidentally, eventually attract some Parliamentary criticism because the Army tended to torment its ex-National Service reservists to a far greater extent.

On the right we have the notional 72 000 *voluntary* reservists of the RAuxAF and RAFVR. I say 'notional' because there were never anything like 72 000. In the event of an emergency the auxiliary units would be embodied and take their places in the front line. VR personnel would be used, as required, to reinforce any formed units, regular or auxiliary.

The Supplementary List[2] was a rather amorphous arrangement whereby ex-wartime officers, that is mostly ex-wartime VR, could

[2]The early post-war Supplementary List (confusingly, the same term was used between 1957 and 1970 to denote regular officers who were not on the General List, ie those serving on terms which offered employment but little prospect of significant advancement) more or less reinstated an arrangement that had been established in 1938 as the RAF Ex-Officers Emergency Reserve. The volunteer members of the pre-war scheme were generally too old for flying duties (bearing in mind that practically all officers of that era were pilots) but were prepared to serve in any other capacity. The pre-war scheme was brought to a close by WW II, its successor by the Reserve Forces Act of 1954.

	Pilots	**Navs**	**Sigs**	**Total**
Officers	1278	98	32	1408
Aircrew	680	44	50	774
WAAF	35	0	0	35
Totals	**1993**	**142**	**82**	**2217**

Fig 2. RAFVR strength Sep 48 (selected flying personnel only).

register their willingness to be recalled in an emergency. Established in 1947, it was an entirely optional undertaking and involved no training commitment.

You will recall that the early post-war calculations had indicated a need for some 760 aeroplanes to get all of the VR aircrew airborne (strictly speaking, only the pilots, navigators and signallers) and possibly for elementary flying training as well. The requirement did not materialise on quite such a large scale, for two reasons. First, it had been decided not to offer *ab initio* instruction and, secondly, because recruiting never came anywhere near the target.

Figure 2 shows the manning position, with respect to those aircrew categories requiring flying experience, at the end of September 1948, at which stage nineteen of the planned twenty-five Reserve Flying Schools had opened. This was after only eighteen months, of course, so one could hardly have expected the quota to have been completely filled but the 2000-odd shown here represented only 15% of the more than 15 000 pilots, navs and signallers that were required. The fact was that people simply were not flocking to the Reserve Centres in the numbers that had been hoped for; the situation with regard to groundcrew was even more disappointing.

Another interesting feature of this table is that it includes female pilots, reflecting an innovation sanctioned by the Secretary of State (Philip Noel-Baker) in June 1947. The intake was limited to 200, all of whom were already to have logged at least 100 hours solo (later reduced to 50). As you can see, there were thirty-five of them by September 1948 but there were never more than about seventy.

We now need to consider the implications of the revised arrangements for conscription which were introduced by the National Service Act (1948) and their impact on Reserve Forces. For simplicity, and because we tend to perceive them to be the most critical (not to say limiting) factor, I am going to continue to concentrate on flying personnel, particularly pilots.

In the immediate post-war years the VR and AAF had been manned by experienced wartime veterans. They were on four- or five-year engagements, however, so from 1951 onwards they would start to thin out and, as we have already seen in the case of the VR, they had never actually signed on in sufficient numbers anyway. This recruiting underachievement was also apparent among the auxiliaries and it was a reasonable assumption that any wartime pilot who had not been moved to sign on by 1950 was not going to.

The solution to the shortage of reserve pilots was to train National Servicemen provided that they undertook to fulfil their subsequent reserve obligation via membership of the VR or, better still, with an auxiliary squadron. It was eventually agreed that 300 conscripts would be selected for flying training annually, of which, allowing for contemporary wastage rates, slightly more than half might be expected to qualify for a pilots badge.

But there was a major snag in that it took eighteen months to train a pilot to 'wings' standard whereas full-time National Service was to be for only a year. Some consideration was given to awarding badges at the end of the basic phase but this was vetoed on the grounds that it would represent a lowering of standards (although that is when badges were awarded before the war and, indeed, when they are awarded today). That would leave National Service pilots passing to the reserve in the exalted rank of Pilot IV (a quasi-corporal) and without a flying badge.

The solution to this problem was the Preliminary Flying Badge (the PFB) which was introduced specifically for VR aviators who could demonstrate their professional skills to the basic level. In the event the period of full-time service had been extended to eighteen months before the new National Service Act actually came into force in January 1949 so most pilots would have been able to complete all three phases of flying training to qualify for a full-blown RAF pilots badge. This would not have been true in every case, however, perhaps due to sickness or injury, and there were the part-trained direct entrants who also needed to be catered for, ex-UAS members for instance, so there was still a residual requirement for the preliminary badge within the VR.

Twenty-three year-old Cadet Pilot Joan Lockwood, who qualified for her PFB with the RAFVR in January 1953.

Furthermore, there were the female VR pilots, some of whom were very experienced and who would certainly have been able to demonstrate flying skills to, at least, the *basic* level and who would thus have qualified for the PFB. Indeed the PFB was the first RAF-sponsored flying badge that women were entitled to wear. The pilot version was introduced in September 1949 and it survives today in the context of the UASs. Corresponding emblems were authorised for the four non-pilot categories but I have yet to find evidence for any of these having ever been awarded, although a handful of navs may have qualified at Cambridge UAS in the mid-1950s (*but see p177* - **Ed**).

There were, incidentally, fifty-eight women VR pilots in February 1953; thirteen of them had qualified for their PFBs. The exploitation of National Service to provide pilots continued to be of considerable significance to our non-regular forces, but to the auxiliaries as much as to the VR so I will leave Tony Freeman to pick up this trail.

In the meantime, serious reservations had begun to be expressed about the practical value of VR aviators in general and of the RFSs in particular. Some of this dissatisfaction arose from within the ranks, where there was a growing sense of frustration among some VR pilots. Many of those who already had their 'wings' resented the constraints imposed by the Tiger Moth (or the later Chipmunk) while those without could make no progress.

For instance, while a female pilot, like Joan Lockwood, would doubtless have been proud to wear her PFB, it did not really represent all that much of a milestone in her case because she had already been flying for six years and held a Private Pilots Licence and a twin-engine rating. Further progress up the military ladder was not an option for her, however, because, leaving aside the question of gender, an RFS provided no access to the crucial Prentice/Harvard sequence. And completion of the Prentice/Harvard course was the only way to gain one's 'wings'.

This internal discontent was amplified by a sniping campaign sponsored by the Secretariat, F.11 to be specific; this began in 1948 and went on for at least two years. Its effectiveness was enhanced by the fact that it was conducted against a backdrop of poor reserve recruiting. No 4 RFS at Brough had already folded due to lack of uptake; Nos 20 and 21 were never opened and plans to raise the total to thirty had been abandoned.

We need not debate the reasons for the recruiting shortfall but it was substantially reduced in 1949 by moving the goalposts. Instead of requiring 20 000 VR aviators, it was decided that we needed only 13 000, 4500 of whom were to be pilots. In mid-1950 the VR's critics fired another broadside which pointed out that, even in an emergency, it was unlikely to yield *competent* reinforcements in less than six months, possibly as long as a year, and noting that the wartime veterans were probably getting a bit too long in the tooth anyway.

In point of fact a very experienced wartime pilot aged, say, 27 when he joined the VR in 1947 would have been only 30 years old in 1950, so what were the critics getting at? It is quite clear that there was a general consensus that 30 was a bit old for a pilot, yet I have flown with 50 year-old Vulcan pilots and I know of 50 year-old Phantom drivers. So what lay behind this observation? I think that it arose from the fact that in 1950 we had less than forty year's experience of military aviation from which to draw conclusions.

WW I had been fought by 20 year-old pilots who were succeeded by the 20 year-old short service officers of the 1920s and '30s so the average age stayed at 20-25. When WW II began even the oldest of Cranwell graduates would have been only in their late 30s. As squadron leaders or junior wing commanders most of them were either dead or group captains within a year or so and the 1939-45 war was fought by another batch of 20 year-olds. The cumulative experience of military aviation ever since 1914 clearly showed that pilots were people who were less than 25 years of age. QED. At 30 you were pushing the limit and that did colour perceptions when the staffs were considering reserves and auxiliaries (*and* regulars) in the early 1950s.

As the Americans were soon to learn in Korea, however, the seasoned veterans of WW II were more than capable of holding their own in combat. Today, of course, we are accustomed to grizzled and balding 'specialist aircrew' (or, to use the latest jargon, 'professional aviators') but the RAF did not fully embrace that concept until 1970 by which time we had learned that there really was life after 40!

YEAR	CATEGORY	DURATION
1951	Auxiliary Fighter[1] Squadrons (2300 men)	3 months
1951	1000 VR Pilots[2]	3 months
1951	200 QFIs	18 months
1951	8600 Class G Airmen	15 days
1951	4200 Class H Airmen	15 days
1952	5000 Class G Airmen	15 days
1952	6000 Class H Airmen	15 days
1953	10000 Class H Airmen	15 days

Notes:
1. Not No 622 Sqn or the Auster units.
2. 75 hrs Tiger Moth to Vampire conversion via Harvard and Spitfire.

Fig 3. Reserves called up during the Korean War.

But enough of demographics. Back to the reserves. How did they respond to the Korean crisis? As shown by Figure 3, there was a limited activation of the auxiliary squadrons in 1951, involving some 2300 men (it would have been more like 3200 if they had been fully manned) plus the recall of about 1000 VR pilots who were given an intensive twelve-week/75-hour course which took them from their customary Tiger Moths via Harvards and Spitfires to Vampires – but then it was back to Tiger Moths again, hence the frustration factor. This activity in the voluntary sector was supplemented by the selective recall between 1951 and 1953 of more than 30 000 Class G and H reservists who were required to report for 15-days of refresher training in order to ensure that the Control and Reporting System would function.

I should, perhaps, point out that, in wartime, the Control and Reporting System was supposed to have been manned largely by auxiliaries and it was the failure to meet auxiliary recruiting targets that had made it necessary to call out these 'G- and H-Men'. As is so often the case with air force history, however, we tend to overlook some factors because we like to focus on pilots, and, in dealing with reserves today, I have been tending to do this myself. We should understand, however, that pilots represent only the icing on a very large cake, and, in the context of reserves, the National Service scheme had ensured that there would

Help keep Britain "ON TOP" in the air

To keep Britain 'on top' in the air is to safeguard world peace. That is a responsibility not only of the R.A.F. but also of its Auxiliaries and Reserves, the men and women who choose to spend a little of their spare time serving so great an end. If *you* are both air-minded and peace-minded, you will find this a grand part-time job. It is at once exciting and rewarding.

ROYAL AUXILIARY AIR FORCE

Flying squadrons (fighter and air observation post) (men and women), light ack-ack Regiment Squadrons (men), and Fighter Control (radar) Units (men and women) which train as *self-contained* city or county units.

Certain Auxiliaries and Reservists do their summer training overseas

R.A.F. VOLUNTEER RESERVE

For aircrew or ground duties (men and women) who train at local Reserve Centres and Flying Schools *as individuals* (annual camp only if living too far from a Centre).

TO: AIR MINISTRY (A.P.65) ADASTRAL HOUSE, LONDON, W.C.2
Please send details (pay, allowances, uniform, etc.) of R.A.F. Auxiliaries and Reserves.

NAME ....

ADDRESS ....

Experience not essential but ex-R.A.F. men and women especially welcome.
(If ex-R.A.F. give Rank, Trade and No.)

If you are between 14 and 17—and keen—join the **AIR TRAINING CORPS**

Fig 4. *This RAuxAF/RAFVR recruiting advertisement from 1950 was clearly aimed at tradesmen, rather than pilots.*

	POTENTIALLY OPERATIONAL			SEMI-OP	NON-OP	TOTALS
	Op	Short OCU	Full OCU	Refresh + Full OCU			
Pilots	0	44	19	1361	954	1363	3743
Navs	0	10	535	131	15	122	813
Sigs	0	2	417	189	21	74	703
Eng	0	3	97	N/A	2	0	102
AG	0	3	135	N/A	0	0	138
Totals	**0**	**62**	**1103**	**1681**	**992**	**1559**	**5497**

Fig 5. Classification of RAFVR Aircrew in mid-1952

always be sufficient pilots to fill the cockpits of the Meteors and Vampires of the auxiliary squadrons. Reserve recruiting was not about pilots; it was about airmen (and airwomen) in ground trades. My point is made, I think, by the typical Auxiliary/VR recruiting advertisement from 1950 at Figure 4. This has clearly been aimed at tradesmen: fitters; armourers; radar mechanics; teleprinter operators; raid plotters; Regiment gunners and so on. *This* is where the problems lay.

That having been said, despite the expansion of the regular air force, by 1952 the shortfall in VR aircrew had been further reduced by another goalpost-moving exercise. Instead of the 13 000 of 1949 we now needed only 7600 aircrew, although we were still running light, as there were only about 6000 on strength.

In June of that year the Auxiliary and Reserve Forces Committee assessed the currency of VR aircrew. Owing to the unavailability of some records about 500 of these men were not included in the survey, but the approximately 90% sample reflected in Figure 5 was more than enough to indicate the overall state of play.

In short, no VR aircrew could be regarded as being immediately fit for operations but 2846 (the third, fourth and fifth columns) could be brought up to scratch within a week to six months. 992 'fell short of Command operational requirements' although some could probably have been salvaged and/or been employed on non-operational duties. The remaining 1559 would take more than six months to recover and would, even then, probably have been fit only for secondary roles.

Almost extinct by 1952, this Tiger Moth was with No 18 RFS.

In the sense that it was a health check, this 1952 survey produced a couple of other interesting observations. First, it was noted that the replacement of Tiger Moths by Chipmunks was virtually complete. This had permitted proper instrument flying to be done and some 760 VR pilots, which would have been about one in five, now held an instrument rating with this proportion increasing steadily. It has to be said, however, that, while the Chipmunk certainly represented an advance over the Tiger Moth, VR pilots were still left at the starting gate because the RAF was moving on from the Prentice/Harvard to the Provost/Vampire. Furthermore, it was already considering introducing all-through jet training and this would have been done before the end of the decade. All of which was tending to make the RFSs increasingly irrelevant.

The second observation was to do with manning; it was noted that the original 1947-vintage volunteers were reaching the end of their engagements and that they were not being replaced on a one-for-one basis, although the RFSs were being kept reasonably busy with ex-short service regular and ex-National Service aircrew fulfilling their reserve obligations.

By this time the Chiefs of Staff were coming to grips with the implications of the fact that, somewhat inconveniently, and probably ten years earlier than they should have done, the Soviets had detonated a nuclear device in 1949. It would take some time for this notional capability to become a substantial threat but it was clear that the atom bomb had invalidated the current 1930s-style defence posture which was predicated on maintaining regular forces sufficient only to blunt an initial *conventional* thrust while large reserve forces were mobilised and deployed. WW III could well be unbelievably violent and short. Or it might still be prolonged, but the new *short* option made it necessary to review the whole question of reserves.

So far as the air force was concerned, it was, as ever, preoccupied with the provision of aircrew and the upshot was the Baker-Carr Report of January 1953. Nearly thirty pages long, including ten annexes of fairly dense maths to do with utilisation rates, aircrew:aircraft ratios; peace versus war establishments, forecast wastage rates and so on, I could not possibly summarise it in a couple of minutes but I will highlight one or two of the conclusions which it drew.

First, although he was obliged to make appropriate references to 'reserves', Air Cdre John Baker-Carr had found this term to be unhelpful and he introduced the concept of First and Second Reinforcements, and these terms became part of the *patois* of the mid-1950s.

The First Reinforcement addressed the case of a short-notice/short-duration WW III, and, as an aside, it also provided the original rationale for the identification of Reserve (or 'Shadow') Squadrons as additional potential units. First Reinforcement personnel were to be those who were *immediately* available to bring the front line up to strength and to replace initial losses. That meant that they had to have had at least one operational tour of experience (which ruled out National Servicemen) and that they had been in current flying practice within the last twelve months. In effect, this meant serving regular aircrew who had been assigned to instructional duties or ground appointments within the previous twelve months, plus those who had recently been discharged into the RAFRO or Class E.

The people in the Second Reinforcement, which was intended to cater for a more prolonged conflict, could be less capable and up to four years out of practice so this group included ex-National Service aircrew in the RAFVR and Class H, plus the balance of the regulars serving on ground tours. Because of their limited experience and/or the interval that had elapsed since they had last been in current flying practice, however, they would take a finite time to mobilise and/or refresh. Nevertheless, it was calculated that the Second Reinforcement would probably provide an adequate cushion over the twelve to eighteen months that would be required before a completely new generation of aircrew started to

	TOTAL AVAILABLE[1]	NUMBERS REFRESHED[2]
Pilots	2720	332
Navs	620	80
Sigs	550	65
Eng	470	141
AG	680	164
Totals	**5040**	**782**

Notes:
1. First *and* Second Reinforcements.
2. First Reinforcement only.

***Fig 6.** RAFVR aircrew refreshed via attachments to regular squadrons Jan-Oct 53*

materialise, presumably from an expanded national, or a reinvigorated 'empire', air training scheme. Projections raised at the time indicated that by 1957 about 1000 reservists were expected to be in action within a month of the start of the shooting season with another 3200 being drip fed back to the squadrons over the next nine months or so.

One of the key features of Baker-Carr's proposal was that there would be far less continuation training for reservists but what there was was going to be of much higher quality. To keep the First Reinforcement up to scratch, they were to receive periodic, realistic, that is to say operational, refresher training at a level of sophistication far beyond that which could be provided by Chipmunks and Ansons at an RFS. On the other hand, the Second Reinforcement would not be required to maintain currency at all. It followed, therefore, that the RFS flying task would dwindle almost to nothing and that there would be no point in sustaining these units.

Substantial progress was made in the context of providing more representative on-the-job refresher training for the First Reinforcement by attaching reservists to regular squadrons. Figure 6 reflects figures submitted to the Air Council to show the achievement during 1953. As you can see, there were more than 5000 VR aircrew at that time but only about 1000 of these would have been in the *First* Reinforcement so the 780 probably represented close to an 80% success rate in the first ten months of the programme, which was not too bad at all.

An Anson T.21 of No 23 RFS. The daisies in the foreground underline George Ward's comment on the increasing irrelevance of the RFSs.

The Baker-Carr scheme was not perfect, of course; the cost of refresher training must have been considerable and it would have been carried out at the not inconsiderable expense of the disruption caused by the diversion of effort at the receiving unit *and* due to the absences of the trainee from his place of work, including those who were still in uniform, of course. The consequences of implementing wholesale in-service refresher training had been appreciated from the outset, however, and the practice was never taken to extremes.

Finally, Baker-Carr had concluded that the auxiliary squadrons 'can no longer be justified on either operational or economic grounds' and he recommended that they should be disbanded. Of which more anon.

This was strong medicine but it was clearly expected to effect a cure because Air Cdre Baker-Carr got his second star! His Reinforcement Scheme was duly adopted, as was his appreciation of the declining value of the RFSs. In fact, because of the already reduced size of the VR, the Air Council had decided to start running down the RFSs, even before Baker-Carr presented his findings. In a statement to the House in December 1952 the Parliamentary Under-Secretary of State, George Ward, pointed out the increasing irrelevance of continuing to fly RFS Chipmunks and Ansons off grass strips in the jet age at a cost of some £2.5M per year and he announced that seven of these units were to be closed. £2.5M would be something in excess of £40M in today-money, but that still doesn't really provide an adequate comparison, because you wouldn't get much change from your £40M if you bought a single Eurofighter whereas my Dad's £2.5M might have bought him close to three full squadrons of Hunters.

The PUS repeated this exercise in March 1953 when he announced the closure of another seven RFSs and he made another interesting statement in June when he revealed that the RAFVR aircrew requirement was now down to a mere 3200, all but 1000 of them being pilots. In making this reduction incidentally, the Ministry had played the age card again; unless they had Transport Command experience or were QFIs, all VR pilots over 28 years of age had been transferred to the non-flying list.

The closure of the RFSs provoked a fairly robust, but dignified, protest from BALPA. After all, closing these essentially civilian institutions meant the loss of a large number of jobs practically all of which were being held down by ex-RAF men, the groundcrew as well as the 300-or-so flying and nav instructors. The Air Council was sympathetic but the inevitability of the decision was unavoidable and everyone knew it. The overcapacity that had always been there was now becoming more obvious and, under the new Reinforcement Scheme, the schools had, in any case, simply outlived their usefulness. Indeed the remaining RFSs were living on borrowed time and in January 1954 George Ward was on his feet again to announce that they too were to be shut down; the last one closed in July.

The final withdrawal of flying facilities for the RAFVR in 1954, more or less concludes my contribution. With the closure of the Town Centres, RAFVR personnel were organised into numbered (in the 7000-series) Reserve Flights and assigned to specific RAF stations where they were to train, the purpose of these flights being to bring peacetime manning up to full war establishment. In war some 25% of the additional manpower required was expected to be provided by locally engaged VR airmen, the other 75% being recalled Class E (supplemented by Classes G or H) reservists who would be assigned by the Records Office. Some flights were specifically concerned with the Control & Reporting chain while others were intended for civil defence duties (notably fire-fighting), a high profile concern at the time. For a brief period, this was a growth industry and by 1955 Fighter Command alone was sponsoring forty-seven reserve flights.

I have a few loose ends to tie off. You will recall that the ex-wartime Class G men were vulnerable to recall for the duration of an 'emergency' that had been declared as long ago as 1939. Surprisingly enough, that emergency was still deemed to exist until the Reserve Act of 1954 finally declared it to be over. Nevertheless, the 1954 Act took the seamanlike precaution of extending membership of the Class G Reserve so that the 'G-Men' remained subject to recall to meet a real crisis until as late as June 1959 (or the age of 45, whichever was the earlier).

Meanwhile, by 1957, the government had accepted that the UK had been fighting above its weight and that this sort of effort was no longer sustainable. Furthermore, it was becoming increasingly obvious that a short-notice, short-duration WW III could be fought or, better still, prevented only by full-time professional Cold Warriors. Since there would be insufficient time to mobilise, refresh, equip and deploy *expensive* reserve forces, these were all to be drastically reduced in size; a cut back which spelled the end of the station-based Reserve Flight scheme. This had peaked in 1957 when there had been about 300 such flights but by 1962 there were only 120 and the numbers continued to dwindle thereafter.

Then again, conscription, which had been extended to two year's active service in 1950 in response to the Korean crisis, was becoming increasingly unpopular, and thus harder to sustain politically. The last intake was in January 1961. They were discharged into Class H two years later, the Reserve Act of 1959 having made them vulnerable to recall until 30 June 1964.

We can, therefore, regard 1964 as the end of an era in terms of reserve *liability*. So far as *voluntary* reserve service was concerned, however, that era had more or less ended with the rapid run down of the RAFVR in the late 1950s. That is not to say that the VR was completely out of business, of course. There was some residual provision for reservists to fill war appointments and a few specialised units were retained, indeed formed, to handle specific tasks, including a Public Relations Squadron and three specialised Intelligence Squadrons. The RAFVR also continued to provide, as it still does, the umbrella organisation for officers of the ATC and members of the UASs. Nevertheless, from 1960 onwards the RAFVR was a mere shadow of what it had been for the previous twenty years or more.

This was not a reflection on its value, of course, simply a sign of the times.

THE POST-WAR ROYAL AUXILIARY AIR FORCE
Squadron Leader A F Freeman

Tony Freeman joined a RAuxAF FCU in 1958. When it disbanded in 1960, he transferred to the newly-formed No 1 Maritime Headquarters Unit before leaving to pursue family and business interests. He re-enlisted with the Movements Squadron at Brize Norton in 1983. Commissioned in 1985, he was mobilised for the Gulf War in 1991 and subsequently became the unit's OC Ops and Deputy OC. He retired in 2000, having spent the previous five years at Innsworth on a Full Time Reserve Commitment, drafting new regulations for the reserve air forces.

Since I am going to cover fifteen years in half-an-hour you will, I hope, forgive me if I concentrate on the flying squadrons, because they are (or were) the most visible manifestation of the auxiliary presence, the flagship of the force.

By March 1945, it had been decided not to include squadrons with auxiliary number plates in the Target Force for Stage II (the final campaign against Japan). A public statement to this effect was made in July and the last of the nominally AAF squadrons actually disbanded in September. Two months later the Air Ministry wrote to the twenty concerned County Associations with firm proposals to re-establish the squadrons which they had sponsored in the past. This proposal was greeted with some enthusiasm.

As with the pre-war 52-squadron scheme, the new AAF was to constitute an element of the front line but there were certain practical constraints. One was that the AAF contribution should be kept in proportion and not allowed to unbalance the overall force structure. There were, for instance, simply too few photo-reconnaissance and maritime strike units for them to be able to accommodate an AAF element. It was also concluded that the heavy bomber, transport and long-range maritime patrol roles were too complex to be fulfilled by part-time aircrew. Then again, it was intended that AAF squadrons should operate from their home stations, which ruled out light bomber and fighter bomber duties as mobility was an essential characteristic of such squadrons. That did not leave too many options and there were concerns that if all twenty AAF

UNIT	ROLE	PRIMARY EQUIPMENT
500 Sqn	NF	Mosquito NF 30
501 Sqn	DF	Spitfire F.21/22/24
502 Sqn	LB	Mosquito B.25
504 Sqn	LB	Mosquito B.25
600 Sqn	DF	Spitfire F.21/22/24
601 Sqn	DF	Spitfire F.21/22/24
602 Sqn	DF	Spitfire F.21/22/24
603 Sqn	DF	Spitfire F.21/22/24
604 Sqn	DF	Spitfire F.21/22/24
605 Sqn	NF	Mosquito NF 30
607 Sqn	DF	Spitfire F.21/22/24
608 Sqn	LB	Mosquito B.25
609 Sqn	NF	Mosquito NF 30
610 Sqn	DF	Spitfire F.21/22/24
611 Sqn	DF	Spitfire F.21/22/24
612 Sqn	DF	Spitfire F.21/22/24
613 Sqn	DF	Spitfire F.21/22/24
614 Sqn	DF	Spitfire F.21/22/24
615 Sqn	DF	Spitfire F.21/22/24
616 Sqn	LB	Mosquito B.25

Fig 1. Reconstituted AAF as authorised on 10 May 46.

squadrons were assigned to the day fighter role, they would distort the constitution of the air defence force.

The eventual compromise was, as shown at Figure 1: thirteen squadrons of day fighters; three of night fighters and four of light bombers. The AAF was authorised to re-form on this basis. Recruiting was to begin in June 1946 with the force being equipped to cadre scale by the end of July. Cadre scale involved a single nine-aircraft operational flight plus a training flight (to be maintained largely by regular airmen) with half-a-dozen additional aeroplanes, including a couple of Harvards or Oxfords. It was envisaged that all squadrons would be fully manned,

	ESTABLISHMENT	STRENGTH	%AGE
Officers (flying)	180	144	80%
Aircrew	160	96	60%
Officers (ground)	100	72	72%
Airmen	2455	826	34%
Totals	2895	1138	39%

Fig 2. Manning of RAuxAF flying squadrons as at 31 Mar 48.

with a second flight and eighteen operational aircraft, by the end of December 1947.

Before that, however, on 6 September 1947, His Majesty honoured the AAF by granting it the prefix 'Royal' thus making it the *R*AAF. The Australians were a trifle miffed by the hi-jacking of *their* short title by a bunch of Pommie reservists, however, and by the time that the formal announcement of the honour was made in January 1948, the abbreviation had become R *A-u-x* AF.

Meanwhile it had been decided to broaden the spectrum of auxiliary activities. Each flying squadron was now intended have a collocated Light Anti-Aircraft Regiment Squadron and auxiliary man- (and woman) power was to provide the bulk of the Control and Reporting System. Recruiting for the first eight, of an eventual twenty-six, Air Defence Units (later Fighter Control Units) began in February 1947 while twelve of the planned twenty 196-man Regiment squadrons were formed during the year and they too joined the trawl for volunteer manpower.

All of this early post-war enthusiasm turned out to have been a trifle optimistic and many things simply did not happen as planned. No 616 Sqn, for instance, finished up with night fighter Mosquitos, rather than the intended bombers. Nor did they happen as quickly as had been hoped, most of the day fighter squadrons having to make do with old Spitfire 14s or 16s until 1948 when the first post-war models began to be issued.

Nor did the build up take place on anything like the scale that had been anticipated. Recruiting for the flying squadrons did not actually begin until November 1946 and by January 1948 932 airmen had enlisted, representing about 37% of the total requirement, which was not bad, considering that we were only a little over a year into the programme. But there was clearly still a very long way to go. Three months later, however, rather than having improved, the situation was slightly worse and there were actually 106 *fewer* tradesmen than there had been in January, although, as Figure 2 indicates, the position was pretty satisfactory with respect to officers and aircrew.

Meanwhile, as early as April 1946, reservations were being expressed about the level of proficiency that a part-time unit could *realistically* be expected to attain. For example, when asked to specify the types of equipment that should be installed in AAF Mosquitos, DD Bomber Ops, Gp Capt Walter Sheen, had responded that it was not a question that needed to be addressed for at least another year, because it would take that long for occasional weekend flyers to achieve a safe level of competence in routine piloting exercises and in straightforward 'contact' navigation and visual bomb-aiming. Time enough to worry about OBOE and GEE-H once that basic standard had been achieved.

As it happened, such standards never were achieved. Having managed with the odd Harvard and Oxford, the prospective Mosquito units did not begin to receive their operational aeroplanes until mid-1947 and it soon became apparent that the auxiliaries would find these difficult to operate. Having two engines was not a problem but having two crew members was, because they were all too often unable to co-ordinate their individual activities so as to both be available at the same time.

But these were not the only problems and in June 1947 ACAS(Trg), Sir Basil Embry, wrote to Vice-Chief to express his concerns. These were that the auxiliary squadrons were presently living off the fat represented by wartime veterans and that the air force needed to face up to the fact that, once this stock had been depleted it would have to start using inexperienced crews. Since these crews flew relatively infrequently he wanted the pilots to be restricted to day fighter tasks and he had strong reservations about their ability to cope with even this in the future, because the interception game was becoming increasingly complex. Embry recommended biting this bullet and accepting that the most realistic approach would be for the auxiliary squadrons to have no operational role. Instead he wanted them to be equipped with advanced trainers, the aim being to maintain the currency and competence of auxiliary pilots at such a level that they could proceed directly to an OCU in the event of an emergency. If that approach were unacceptable, however, Embry asked that, 'We should at least get rid of the worst present anomaly – the attempts of the AAF to maintain operational standards of efficiency on night fighters and light bombers, which is even now beyond their capabilities.'

One of the reasons why Embry's *key* recommendation was rejected was that the auxiliaries were expected to provide a substantial proportion of the front line. In fact, rather than reducing their operational commitments, in 1949 the Secretary of State, Arthur Henderson, would suggest that there might be advantage in *doubling* the number of auxiliary fighter squadrons to forty. It fell to ACAS(Pol), AVM Douglas Macfadyen, to pour cold water on that one. There were four main objections.

First, convenient and sensible basing arrangements could be provided for only sixteen additional squadrons. Secondly, recruiting for the existing twenty squadrons was far from easy, and the County Associations (who would be responsible for recruiting) saw the potential for only six more units. Thirdly, the post-war auxiliary squadrons were not manned entirely by part-timers and additional units would be expensive in regulars.[1] Finally, like the majority of air marshals, Macfadyen was very aware of the gulf that existed 'between the man who can fly a modern fighter and the skilled pilot who can operate it effectively.' With the experience level declining and the difficulty of the task increasing he foresaw that the value of the auxiliary squadrons 'as front line units will decrease until, in the comparatively near future, the stage will be reached when they can be regarded as no more than a formed reserve.' That being the case, there was little point in creating twenty *more* such units and the idea was dropped.

While Embry's idea of turning the auxiliary squadrons into what amounted to holding pens for *potentially* operational pilots had been rejected, his second wish was granted and the auxiliaries were not obliged to persevere with Mosquitos for much more than a year. By the end of 1948 they had all been phased out in favour of single-seat fighters, still mostly Spitfires but with the odd Vampire beginning to appear, thus making good on a public statement to the effect that the auxiliaries would be equipped with jets during 1948. As was so often the case, this was easier said than done and it was well into 1951 before the RAuxAF disposed of the last of its prop-driven fighters.

---

[1] In 1948 the regular establishment of an auxiliary squadron stood at three officers, five NCOs and thirty-three airmen, a total of forty-one, although HQ Reserve Command had recently submitted a bid for this to be increased to sixty-four.

An Auster AOP 6 of No 663 Sqn at Hawarden in 1956.

Apart from deciding to do away with the Mosquito in 1948 (and thus rendering the auxiliaries a pilot-only force, which eased both recruiting and management problems), another lesson was learned during that year's major air exercise, DAGGER, to which the auxiliaries had been fully committed. During the wash-up it became apparent that the auxiliary squadrons had been 'wired up' wrongly. When they had first been re-established, because they were *non*-regulars, it had seemed logical to place them in Reserve Command along with the VR and the UASs. No doubt that worked well enough from an administrative standpoint but it was the wrong answer for standardising training and operations and DAGGER had demonstrated that the auxiliary squadrons and Fighter Control Units were working to procedures that differed from those used by Fighter Command. Since it was clear that inter-Command co-ordination was not working, it was decided to transfer operational control of the air defence units to Fighter Command and this was done in 1949.

Meanwhile, ever since 1946 the Army had been pressing for the creation of auxiliary squadrons of Austers to support the TA, both as artillery spotters and for field liaison duties. The cost in *air force* manpower (because these units were to be jointly manned by the Army and the RAF, just like regular AOP squadrons) was calculated to be 340 auxiliary personnel and 165 regulars This was sanctioned by the Air Council in 1948 and all five squadrons began to form on a semi-autonomous, dispersed flight basis, during 1949.

There was another innovation in 1950 when it was decided that the auxiliaries should go into the 'trucking' business. The idea was that the independent airlines, of which there were a number in those days, would be invited to sponsor a squadron of Yorks or Vikings. They would have only a handful of RAF-supplied aeroplanes in peacetime but when embodied they would make their own fleets available. As an experiment, Airwork formed No 622 Sqn at Blackbushe and, in anticipation of success, four more potential operators were identified and provisional squadron number plates allotted. Sadly, the idea foundered on the familiar rock of recruiting. By late 1952 the squadron had twenty-three of its intended twenty-six pilots on strength but could field only five radio officers and a solitary air engineer against a requirement for thirteen of each. The reason for the odd pattern of this response was that all commercial flight deck crew had broadly similar social status, whereas the RAF proposed to commission the pilots and palm the rest off with three stripes. The prospective NCOs, who were all ex-RAF of course, had already 'been there, done that' and they were not going to do it again.

There were two reasons why groundcrew failed to respond. First, as had been found in the 1920s, people were disinclined to volunteer to do, over the weekend, precisely the same thing that they had been doing all week. Secondly, they were certainly not prepared to do it for *far* less money. The transport initiative was abandoned in 1953.

I now need to backtrack about five years to register the impact of the National Service Act of 1948. As the previous speaker has explained, when it was first introduced full-time National Service was for eighteen months, just long enough to permit a pilot to acquire his 'wings', but stopping short of the applied stage. Since ex-regulars were no longer joining the auxiliaries in sufficient numbers, it had to be accepted that the bulk of future pilots would have to be conscripts who would agree to discharge their four-year reserve commitment as an auxiliary. Solely to satisfy this requirement, therefore, it was agreed that 300 National Servicemen would be selected for flying training on an annual basis. Since the new system did not start until January 1949, however, the first of these men would not materialise until mid-1950 at which point the Korean War broke out. Full-time National Service was promptly extended to two years and the numbers being inducted for aircrew training were substantially increased. Provided that he did not run into any snags, therefore, a pilot could now complete the entire training sequence *and* yield a few months of productive service at squadron level before passing to the reserve and adequate numbers were expected to

ESTABLISHMENT	STRENGTH	
	1951	**1952**
Fighter Squadrons (20)		
Pilots	340	326	298
Ground	2890	1883	1764
Transport Squadron (1)		
Flying	52	1	26
Ground	112	1	48
Fighter Control Units (26)		
Officers	1401	389	460
Airmen/women	18070	4077	4552
RAF Regt LAA Sqns (12)		
Officers	96	57	65
Airmen	2256	897	1115
AOP Sqns (5)		
Officers*	10	4	5
Airmen	363	142	198

*Most Auster pilots were furnished by the Army, as was a proportion of each squadron's ground element, notably signals staff; these figures reflect only RAuxAF personnel.

***Fig 3.** RAuxAF manning versus establishment as at Feb 51 and Feb 52.*

continue to fly with the auxiliaries for the duration of their remaining obligation, ie for three years.

It did not happen quite like that, at least not in the early stages, and as Figure 3 shows, the manning levels on the fighter squadrons actually got slightly worse in 1951-52. The February 1952 figures in the right hand column, represent about 76% with respect to fighter pilots and only 61% for their groundcrew. Recruiting into other elements of the RAuxAF had improved slightly. I have already discussed the disappointing transport experiment. The FCUs were running at about a quarter of their intended strength while the Regiment and AOP squadrons were at about half. This situation was serious because there had always been reservations over the efficiency of the auxiliaries and there was simply no way that they could be regarded as proficient with manning levels like these.

In 1952 AVM Geoffrey Ambler (the second CO of the pre-war No 609 Sqn, now its Honorary Air Commodore and clearly an 'auxiliary' enthusiast) submitted a lengthy paper suggesting a way of overcoming the manning deficit. He believed that the root of the problem lay in a fundamental incompatibility between 100% conscription and *voluntary* service, in that the former was bound to induce an 'I've already paid' attitude. His solution was predicated on the fact that the fighter squadrons (and his, somewhat emotive, paper dealt solely with these) were a part of the front line and that each of them had been 'embodied' for three months in 1951. On that basis he advocated direct recruiting into the auxiliary air force, permitting it to hand-pick high grade, enthusiastic candidates, particularly ATC cadets, who would then be individually 'embodied' for two years of continuous training. During this time they would learn a trade or be taught to fly, mainly in-house or at dedicated schools, while avoiding most of the shouting and stamping that was associated with conscription. In the process, it was argued, they would become dedicated auxiliaries who would remain loyal to their units and give many years of voluntary service. Ambler's scheme was not practical as it stood (it was too cumbersome and the 'individual embodiment' gambit was fraught with legal difficulties) but from late-1953 the squadrons were granted some say in the pre-selection of National Servicemen, both as pilots and for groundcrew duties, the latter, once trained, spending their productive service with the unit which had sponsored them.

Reference has already been made to the TOP SECRET Baker-Carr Report of 1953. This had concluded, that, because of the limited amount of flying time that was available to an auxiliary pilot, future aeroplanes would be too complex for direct entrants (which would have included conscripts) to handle competently. The squadrons would, therefore, have had to be manned by ex-regulars, which meant that they would really be acting as a refresher facility for the First Reinforcement. Baker-Carr believed that he had identified ways of keeping the First Reinforcement up to speed at a third of the cost of sustaining the twenty auxiliary fighter squadrons and he had recommended that they should all be disbanded. This recommendation was neither endorsed nor dismissed but it was excised from a second edition of the Report which was downgraded to SECRET. The problem was not being swept under the carpet, however. Baker-Carr had said, out loud, several things that had needed to be said and the future of the Royal Auxiliary Air Force became the subject of separate and prolonged study for the next four years.

Before examining the efforts that were made to sustain the auxiliary squadrons there are three other issues that are worthy of a mention. One of the more overt responses to the Korean War was that the fighter squadrons were called up for three months of continuous training in 1951. This stopped short of formal embodiment but it still did not go down well with employers. The level of protest was such that, short of a real emergency, the Air Council resolved not to repeat the exercise before 1955 at the earliest – and they never were called out again.

The second point concerns NATO which had been created in 1949. For planning purposes, SACEUR needed to know what resources were available to him and, against the fairly crude *early* definitions, the Air Ministry had been able to declare all twenty auxiliary squadrons to NATO as being *fully combat capable*. By 1953, however, SHAPE had adopted a more sophisticated approach. Had this been in use in 1952, the auxiliaries would have been Cat A(2) Forces (that is to say fully trained combat units, not specifically assigned to NATO but constituting an element of NATO Force Goals). Unfortunately, under the new rules, the lengthy training sessions of 1951 were too stale to count and the auxiliaries of 1953 had to be classified at Cat B. This meant that (for NATO purposes) they were no longer regarded as being front line units which would have represented a substantial, and I suppose embarrassing, reduction in the UK's contribution to Force Goals.

The third point I want to mention concerns the Fighter Control Units. We have probably forgotten just how labour-intensive the Control and Reporting System was in the early post-war era. It was always intended that most of the personnel required would be auxiliaries, many of them women, but it has to be said that recruiting never came anywhere near meeting the targets. The solution to this was to replace people with technology. This was one of the dynamics behind the, so-called, ROTOR programme which progressively introduced more capable radars and an increasing degree of automation – electronic symbols on cathode ray tubes rather than huge maps with girls pushing model aeroplanes about with a billiard cue. It was still very early days but some idea of the impact of automation can be gained from the fact that in 1951 the demand for auxiliary personnel dropped from more than 15 000 to fewer than 9000.

This eased the manning position considerably but with a strength of under 3000 there was still a 70% deficit.

During 1954 various bodies, including the Air Council and the Auxiliary and Reserve Forces Committee, began to tackle the problem of finding a way to sustain the flying squadrons, for there is no question that that is what most people *wanted* to do. There was a good deal of sentiment involved, but there were sound operational arguments too. Put crudely, the loss of twenty squadrons, whether regular *or* auxiliary, would leave a large hole in the air defence network. Few would have denied that the auxiliaries might need a little intensive practice to make them fully operational but such a grace period had been granted in 1939-40 and it was not (yet) a foregone conclusion that WW III *would* start and end with a nuclear Pearl Harbour; there could well be a lengthy period of tension during which the voluntary services might be mobilised.

The ebb and flow of the arguments would take all day to rehearse so I can do no more than flag up the main events. The Air Council started the ball rolling in May 1954 when it posed eight specific questions to which a committee chaired by DCAS, Air Mshl Tom Pike, attempted to provide answers. The key conclusions drawn by his team were:

a. that only fifteen squadrons should be retained;

b. that all fifteen should be re-armed with Hunters or Swifts;

c. that up to ten of these squadrons should be temporarily mounted on Venoms, pending availability of the swept-wing types; and

d. that the options of Inshore Maritime Patrol, and Search and Rescue were not viable alternatives (because such roles were too unattractive to yield the required manpower, that they would involve aircrew categories that the auxiliaries did not currently employ and that past experience had shown that it was difficult to manage weekend training for multiple crews).

By August the forecast was that only the ten Venom squadrons would be retained and ACAS(Pol), AVM Chilton, was asked to comment on the projected equipment programme. Since it was not really up to the task, Chilton was unenthusiastic about issuing Venoms. In fact, they represented only a short-term solution at best, because the Venom had a life of only 750 flying hours and most of the airframes on offer would be second-hand so the whole force would have run out of steam by 1959 at the latest. Furthermore, Chilton saw little real point in providing the auxiliaries with Hunters and Swifts because, as he pointed out, it would do no more than postpone the inevitable, as there was no way that they would ever be given Lightnings. Nevertheless, by using war reserve aircraft, it would be possible to convert seven squadrons from Venoms to Hunters by mid-1956 and then to mount three more on Swifts. The problem with this approach was that current wastage rates suggested that by mid-1958, twenty-two Hunters and ten Swifts would have been written off. These aeroplanes could not be replaced, of course, because they *were* the replacements. Chilton concluded by recommending the retention of only the seven prospective Hunter squadrons.

Clearly, there were serious reservations over the wisdom of providing the auxiliaries with swept-wing, transonic aeroplanes, especially as it was by now universally accepted (except perhaps at squadron level) that, *in practical terms*, part-time pilots could not be trained on swept-wing aircraft so as to be *immediately* available in war. It was decided not to proceed with the re-equipment programme. Instead, all twenty squadrons were to be retained but reduced to only a training flight of Vampires and/or Meteors. Each squadron was to be affiliated to a regular squadron to which, once the latter had become proficient on Hunters, up to six selected auxiliary pilots would be attached for conversion and familiarisation. In an emergency, these pilots would fly with their *regular* sponsors. In other words, the role of the auxiliary squadrons would be, in effect, to sustain the reserve element of First Reinforcement day fighter pilots. Interestingly, while this outcome had been pretty much Baker-Carr's argument for *dispensing* with the auxiliary fighter squadrons, it was, at the same time, not too far removed from Basil Embry's proposals of 1947.

The new policy was announced in the House by the Minister of Defence, Harold Macmillan, on 1 December 1954 and it must have provoked some heavy-duty lobbying behind the scenes, because a mere three months later, George Ward announced a change of plan. Both the government, and the squadrons, had, he said, found it 'unpalatable' that the auxiliaries should be denied the opportunity to fight as formed units. It had, therefore, been decided to identify a threat with which they might be able to deal. There were two: the Tu-4 (the reverse-engineered Russian adaptation of the B-29) and the possibility of an airborne assault on the UK by troop-carrying transport aircraft. Both arguments were a bit thin, but the anti-invasion commitment in support of the TA sufficed to permit the squadrons to retain their Meteors and Vampires. This restoration of an operational task was, incidentally, in addition to, not instead of, the flying-Hunters-with-the-regulars scheme.

This had been only a temporary stay of execution, however, because the Air Ministry was under increasing pressure to find financial savings and by mid-1955 it had been tacitly accepted that the squadrons would probably *have* to be sacrificed before 1958. Vice-Chief, Air Chf Mshl Sir Ronald Ivelaw-Chapman, eventually grasped the nettle in May 1956 when he circulated a *deliberately* provocative draft paper recommending the disbandment of the flying squadrons. As it did the rounds the case gathered strength, not least because by August the anti-invasion argument had worn so thin that it was virtually transparent. After all, the TA, which the auxiliaries were supposed to be supporting in this endeavour, was being reassigned to assisting the civilian population in the aftermath of a nuclear attack. Furthermore, because of low utilisation rates with the early Hunters, there had been little real progress with training auxiliary pilots as First Reinforcements, this commitment now being defined as 30 swept-wing hours per year for only *two* pilots per squadron plus 100 hours with the parent unit. That was a lot for a part-timer, and that was the root of the problem. It was simply unrealistic to pretend that more than a handful of pilots could maintain a reasonable degree of currency by this means and this at an annual cost of some £4.25M per year (about £65M in today's money). Finally, HQ Fighter Command had tentatively suggested the disbandment of its FCUs and Radar Reporting Units.

To put all of this into some kind of perspective, we must remember that this heart-searching over the auxiliaries was going on against the major review of defence policy which eventually resulted in the Duncan Sandys White Paper of 1957. There simply is not time to deal with *that* today beyond noting that the knives were out for the *regular* squadrons of Fighter Command which left little scope for preserving the auxiliaries. Furthermore, if, as appeared increasingly likely, National Service were to be terminated, this would cut off the primary source of supply of future auxiliary pilots. There was no way out and, at a meeting held on 13 September 1956, after considering Vice-Chief's final paper, which by now advocated the disbandment of the entire auxiliary organisation, not

Sad, but inevitable, redundant RAuxAF Meteor F.8s (this one had belonged to No 615 Sqn) awaiting the breaker's axe at No 12 MU.

just the flying squadrons, the Air Council approved its recommendations. The PM eventually endorsed this decision at the end of December.

While it may provide little consolation, I should perhaps make the point that the air force was not suffering alone; the other Services were experiencing similar cuts, not least the RNVR which was losing all ten of *its* flying squadrons.

On 16 January 1957, a letter was sent to all AOCinCs announcing the disbandment of: all twenty-five flying squadrons; the twelve Regiment squadrons; eight of the FCUs; one Radar Reporting Unit and the Air Intelligence Unit. All flying was to cease *immediately* and all units were to have been closed by 10 March. The War Office had lodged an appeal on behalf of the Auster units on the grounds that they were needed to support the two TA Divisions which were earmarked for BAOR. The Air Council pointed out that the TA was most unlikely even to get across the Channel in WW III and the Army conceded the point.

Manning difficulties with regulars meant that the remaining FCUs and one Radar Reporting Unit actually soldiered on until 1960 when they too were closed down. 1960 would, therefore, have seen the total eclipse of the auxiliaries had it not been for the timely formation of four Maritime Headquarters Units. These were followed by the reinstatement of selected Regiment Squadrons from 1979 onwards and the auxiliaries subsequently branched out into other fields, including Movements, Aeromedical Evacuation and Operations Support, in which roles it still operates today.

RECOLLECTIONS OF A REGULAR WITH A POST-WAR RAuxAF FIGHTER SQUADRON

Air Commodore J C 'Ian' Atkinson

Ian Atkinson joined the RAF via Cranwell in 1947. His first flying tour was on Brigands from which he progressed via Vampires to Canberras. Career highlights included command of No 17 Sqn, RAF Luqa and AHQ Gibraltar. Since his retirement in 1983 he has worked for and/or with RAFA and the Eastern Wessex TAVRA and he was Director of the Air League 1990-95.

My experience of the post-war Royal Auxiliary Air Force was that of the regular adjutant of one of the ten Vampire Squadrons, No 613 (City of Manchester) Sqn, based at RAF Ringway adjoining Manchester airport from which we flew. All squadrons will have differed in some respect, but much of what I have to say will be common ground.

The Vampire squadrons were all singly based and mostly on other than fighter stations, many flying from joint-user airfields. The ten Meteor squadrons were nearly all located on fighter stations, sometimes paired and often alongside RAF squadrons all on the eastern side of the country, the exceptions being Nos 610 (County of Cheshire) and 611 (West Lancashire) Sqns forming a wing at RAF Hooton Park on the Wirral within Western Sector. The air assets of Western Sector were entirely auxiliary with No 613 Sqn, together with No 502 (Ulster) Sqn at RAF Aldergrove and No 605 (County of Warwick) Sqn, forming a second wing at RAF Honiley, No 605 Sqn's base and where the Wing Leader, a regular wing commander, presided. Western Sector's HQ was at Broughton Hall near Preston and was largely auxiliary manned, as were the three GCI stations near Nantwich, Lytham St Anne's and Bishops Court in Northern Ireland.

RAF Ringway had been designed and built to a very high standard, also paid for, by Manchester Corporation in 1939-40 and then leased back to the Air Ministry, a possibly unique arrangement. In my time it was a 63 Gp, Home Command station providing backing for No 613 Sqn, a 12 Gp unit, and other units such as No 1952 (AOP) Flt of No 663 Sqn with their Auster 6s and later on No 3613 (City of Manchester) Fighter Control Unit.

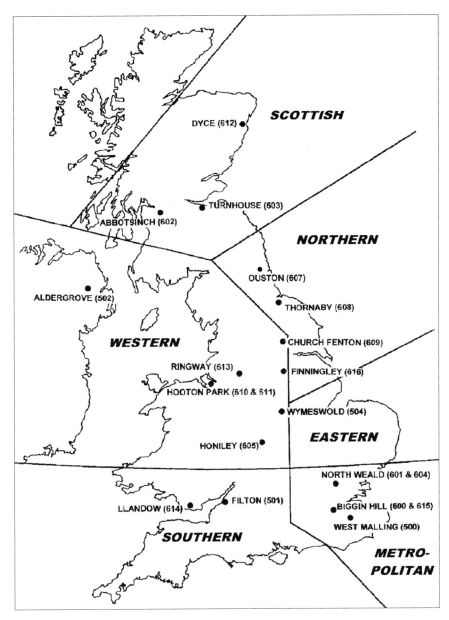

Sector boundaries and peacetime basing of RAuxAF fighter squadrons in the mid-1950s, at which stage Southern and Metropolitan Sectors were within 11 Gp and the rest of the UK within 12 Gp.

No 613 Sqn was the last of the auxiliary units to be formed early in 1939, there being no suitable airfield until Ringway became available the previous year. Equipped with Lysanders and venerable Hawker Hectors in the army co-operation role it flew initially from Odiham and experienced its baptism of fire over Calais in May 1940; one Hector was lost. The squadron was re-equipped with Tomahawks in 1941 and Mustang Is in 1942 for fighter reconnaissance, until re-roled finally for low level intruder operations in 2nd TAF with the Mosquito VI. Of the many low level operations undertaken, and flown mostly from Lasham, the most noteworthy were the attacks on the *Gestapo* Central Records Registry in the Hague in April 1944 and the *SS* barracks at Egletons near Limoges in August that year. The squadron finished the war at Cambrai/Epinoy where it was renumbered as No 69 Sqn. No 613 Sqn was reformed at Ringway in 1946, equipped successively with Spitfires 16 and 22 and in 1951 with ten Vampire FB 5s, two Meteor T.7 trainers and the use of a Chipmunk.

The squadron's auxiliary strength was made up of eighteen officer pilots, nine ground branch officers and up to 150 airmen with a good level of experience. We were fortunate to be able to draw on the wealth of engineering and allied industries in the Manchester area and benefited from the gratuitous publicity gained from flying from a civil airport with its customary weekend onlookers; I do not recall that recruiting was a problem. The regular cadre comprised myself as Adjutant, with oversight of the squadron in the absence of the CO and Flight Commanders, and sharing with the Training Officer the flying and operational training task. The Technical Officer supervised all engineering matters on the squadron and station, assisted by auxiliary engineering and armaments specialists. Our establishment of some fifty RAF tradesmen provided essential continuity, covering the second line engineering task and training support. The CO, Sqn Ldr J B Wales OBE DFC TD was a wartime fighter Squadron Commander and one of the team of Avro test pilots at Woodford. The two Flight Commanders and roughly half of the pilots had wartime, or immediately post-war, RAF experience with the balance being National Service entrants, a number of whom had flown with Manchester University Air Squadron. Last, but certainly not least, was our Honorary Air Commodore, Sir Roy Dobson CBE, the Chairman and Managing Director of Avro and a prominent figure in the Manchester

No 613 Sqn groundcrew tending to the needs of a Vampire at Ringway.

scene. His approach was very much 'hands on' and he gave tremendous encouragement to the squadron as well as practical support.

Flying took place at weekends and sometimes during the Thursday training evenings. With Ringway's proximity to the centre of Manchester, we dispensed with a town headquarters, thus all squadron activities, military and social, were centred on the station permitting flexibility in programming as well as making for a close-knit squadron community. Flying from a civil airport presented no difficulty, given the modest level of civilian traffic in those days. The controllers were used to handling fighters; two were, in fact, auxiliaries. Exit and entry to the airfield was via a special VFR low level lane. In bad weather, and being Manchester, there was plenty of that, we used a special climb out lane to clear the control zone and recovered with a straight descent from overhead Shrewsbury, feeding into the Ringway GCA.

The flying programme followed the Fighter Command training syllabus, taking account of exercise commitments and any local tasking such as exercises with the TA or Observer Corps, and would be drawn up by the CO in conjunction with the Flight Commanders, the Training

Officer and myself, all authorising officers. It would cover the usual spectrum of general handling, formation, low flying and instrument and night flying, with the emphasis on fighter tactics, practice interceptions with cine gun analysis of the attacks and live firing. The latter would be undertaken by deploying to RAF Valley and towing the target banners with our own Meteors or a Mk 8 provided from Hooton Park. A more flexible alternative was to fly the target banners from Ringway using a towline over Liverpool Bay.

I can only recall one mishap with this arrangement when the banner became detached from the tug and draped itself over the roof of a nearby dwelling, to be hailed by the local press as 'the thing from outer space'. Prompt action was called for and the most plausible auxiliary officer was despatched, armed with flowers and chocolates from the squadron fund, to placate the householder and spin skilfully around the question of compensation. I believe that the incident was, in fact, amicably resolved without undue delay.

From time to time we would operate as a wing, flying from Honiley, operating under sector control and usually during major air defence exercises. Squadron lore had it that it always rained at Honiley on a wing weekend and Exercise DIVIDEND in mid-July 1954 was no exception. The weather was abysmal, with a low cloud base and the forecast no better, but it was a major exercise and so up the wing went, breaking cloud at 31 000 feet only to be informed by sector that there was neither trade nor diversions. The recovery, with a now much reduced cloud base, had its moments of excitement with a host of Vampires jockeying for position in the circuit to land.

Occasionally the wing would foregather at Ringway or Aldergrove for any special tasking that had come up, or just to experience the different flying environments and the resident squadron's hospitality.

The high point of the year was the fifteen day's continuous training or summer camp. Attendance was mandatory in order to qualify for the annual auxiliary bounty, which was also dependent on a satisfactory attendance record during the year. In practice this was usually met with some, especially pilots, putting in additional spells of full time attendance. Any laggards could be shown the door after customary warnings.

Summer camps served to concentrate the squadron, affording the benefits of continuous training and the opportunity for intensive air firing

No 613 Sqn's Summer camp in 1952 was at Ta'Qali.

practice, as well as the benefit of operating in a different environment. They were highly popular, especially the overseas camps, and the Malta camp at Ta'Qali in 1952 particularly so. The 1953 camp, held at 2nd TAF's crowded Armament Practice Station at Sylt in the Frisian Islands, provided concentrated gunnery training in a very different setting, though not without its attendant amenities including the notorious Abyssinia Beach. We had a productive and satisfying camp at Thorney Island the following year and then returned to the Mediterranean in 1955, to Gibraltar with its unique operating environment, for more concentrated gunnery. A bonus was participation in a joint exercise with the French, deploying to Oran to fly with the resident French Air Force Mistral squadron (Vampires with a Nene engine) in attacking elements of the French fleet. Shortly after I left in 1956, the squadron experienced its final summer camp, held appropriately at Thornaby, the squadron's designated war deployment base.

Looking back, we enjoyed our flying but took it seriously; high standards were expected and indiscipline was certainly not tolerated. Membership of the squadron was sought after and we had pride in ourselves and our good standing locally.

To complete the picture of life at Ringway, it also included the customary formal inspections, Battle of Britain celebrations and a variety of annual social events. We enjoyed close links with the City of Manchester and our TA colleagues in the East Lancashire area. Once a year the officers of the reserve flying squadrons, both light and dark blue, in Western Sector would get together for a convivial evening, usually at Chester and at Christmas an all-ranks dinner would be held in Manchester with the Honorary Air Commodore present. Saturday evenings normally involved a descent on one or other of the hostelries of the Cheshire countryside. RAF Ringway itself offered good facilities for all ranks with the advantage for many of being a comparatively short distance from their homes.

Well, how effective were we? We reckoned to hold our own, compared with other auxiliary squadrons in terms of experience and proficiency and felt that we were, basically, the equal of a regular squadron whilst acknowledging the need for a short, intensive period to work up to full time operating efficiency. That said, we all recognised that we were flying obsolescent aircraft – a Vampire could not overhaul a Canberra in an interception – and that re-equipment was highly desirable if we were to maintain our worth in the future. I like to think, nevertheless, that we gave good value for money at the time.

The disbandment, when it came in 1957, was received with profound regret tinged with realism. The City marked the squadron's achievements with the presentation of an illuminated scroll at a ceremonial parade on 2 March with a farewell flypast passing overhead. Much later, on 9 May 2000, a memorial plinth was unveiled by the Lord Mayor in the memorial garden outside Terminal One at the airport, with the Queen's Colour of the Royal Auxiliary Air Force being paraded for the occasion. As with many squadrons, the memory is kept alive through an active squadron association.

THE RAuxAF REGIMENT
Flight Lieutenant Shane Guy

Shane Guy's primary career involved the Diplomatic Service and university administration but, in his 'spare time', he also served with either the RAuxAF or the ROC between 1958 and 1995. As an auxiliary he saw service with a Fighter Control Unit, a Maritime Headquarters Unit and a Regiment Squadron. Other civic duties have included ten years as a JP and three on a prison Board of Visitors.

I present this memoir with some diffidence, since I am neither a remembrancer nor an historian. This is a personal, rather than a formal, paper; there are many distinguished members of the Royal Auxiliary Air Force who would be far more qualified than me to present the latter. Furthermore, twenty minutes can hardly do justice to such exciting subject matter.

To understand how I come to be here today one needs first to know how I came to be a rather elderly 'Rock Ape' in 1979. I was a member of the Royal Auxiliary Air Force until the end of the implementation of the 1957 Sandys White Paper in 1961. Subsequently, I was a member of my university's Military Education Committee and of, what is now termed, the Reserve Forces and Cadets Association for the North West of England and the Isle of Man. I maintained a close informal connection with the RAF as an honorary member of the University Air Squadron. Consequently I was aware of discussions on the reorganising and restructuring of RAF Reserves in the 1970s; indeed I had even contributed to a small extent myself via membership of a Working Party examining one aspect of these proposals. As a former auxiliary I was keen to be more directly involved. From my slightly privileged position, my letter of application arrived at one of the first pilot units (the RAF's pun, not mine) prior to the arrival of the first CO to be appointed.

The RAF Regiment and the RAuxAF Regiment 1942-57

The RAF Regiment was formed as a corps within the Royal Air Force in 1942 following the Taylor Report, a Joint RAF/Army study. The initial raw material was provided by 35 000 RAF ground gunners and the Air

Ministry's Directorate of Ground Defence, which had been formed in 1940. The formation being new (although, were this an academic paper, I would be bound to point out the antecedents provided by the Iraq and Aden Levies and the armoured car companies) there were no embodied auxiliary units. The Regiment's initial role was to provide ground and short range air defence for airfields and other sensitive installations. This was subsequently extended to include the capture and holding of enemy, particularly advanced, airfields.

The concept was successful. The *élan* of the new units was such that they rapidly acquired additional responsibilities, partly because of the flexibility of their 'gunners', as airman members were known. Many transferred from other RAF trades seeking more vigorous action and took with them a level of education not always found among infantry conscripts. The Regiment's gunners were required to be familiar with a variety of infantry roles and their advanced skills levels and flexibility led to their being employed in the field far more widely than had originally been contemplated. Army-style khaki uniforms were worn, although ranks and their markings were of the RAF. For the first few years the Commandant General and some senior officers were seconded from the Army. Operational formations were designated as flights, squadrons and wings and, whilst their concepts of operations had been clearly designed to support the RAF, for the purpose of rough comparison it would not be inappropriate to equate these formations to platoons, semi-independent companies and battalions.

The concept of 'The Regiment', born in response to a critical need, survived the peace and when the Auxiliary Air Force was re-established in 1946 it was decided that it should include twenty Regiment squadrons, although only twelve were actually formed. Each was to be associated with a flying squadron and carry the same local affiliation in its name. All were to be LAA squadrons armed with the Bofors L40/60 gun. The first four units formed on 1 May 1947, a fifth on 1 October and the remainder on 1 December. Some shared their Town HQ premises with their parent flying squadron.

Recruiting varied from area to area [this was, perhaps, in part the reason for the redesignation of No 2604 (County of Middlesex) Sqn as No 2600 (City of London) Sqn on 1 June 1949 and for its relocation from Stanmore Park to Biggin Hill] and the history of the RAF Regiment notes that the operational capability of the squadrons could not be uniformly guaranteed on mobilisation. A letter survives from the then CO of No 2502 (Ulster) Sqn in which he bitterly complains of the squadron's being housed in leaky Nissen huts, which, given that part of the world, would certainly have put a damper on things.

In the early 1950s the Bofors L40/60 was nearing the end of its useful operational life and the decision was taken to withdraw it from service. As a consequence, in 1953 it was decided to re-role the RAuxAF Regiment units as field squadrons.

Alas this did not save them and on 10 March 1957, in common with the flying squadrons, they were disbanded. Indeed the future of the RAF Regiment as a whole was thrown into doubt with the disbanding of twenty-eight regular squadrons and eleven regular wing headquarters.

The Royal Auxiliary Air Force Regiment 1979

In March 1979 CAS announced the formation of three new RAuxAF units. Although discussions concerning the expansion of the auxiliary organisation had been under way for some time, this was the first public announcement that the bellwether units were to be Regiment squadrons.

In May it was announced that the new units were to be located at Scampton, Honington and Lossiemouth. Progress was swift. A press release was issued on 16 May and RAF Scampton reported that it was having the first signs made on 1 June. On 15 June it was reported that the CO had arrived and the unit officially opened for business on 1 July. In August a meeting, followed by supper in the Mess, was organised for potential officers. The first training event took place in September when a group photograph was taken. The total number in uniform and on parade, including the Station Commander, was twenty-five; almost a flight!

Such rapid progress was indicative of the enthusiasm with which the RAF Regiment had embraced the auxiliary concept and of the ease with which new recruits fitted in and 'retreads' resumed their familiar functions in the field.

As these were pilot units it had been decided that there would be no increase in the Regiment's regular training establishment to cater for the new squadrons, all of which would, therefore, have to conduct their own training in-house on a self-help basis. The training needs for officers had been under discussion at Branch and Command level since early June and the first stage of agreement was effectively reached on 19 September, when it was agreed that those who had not previously completed IOT should attend the first modules of the SERE course at Cranwell. Medicals took place at the Central Medical Establishment during the first week in October and Commissioning Boards, where these were necessary, for those joining the Scampton squadron, on 8 November. The first squadron training weekend, visited by senior representatives from the Depot, was the first weekend of December and carried out at Bellerby Camp on the Catterick ranges. Amazingly, there were complaints that the process was taking too long, and that certain aspects needed to be speeded up.

The establishment and scaling of equipment for the auxiliary squadrons was similar to that of their regular counterparts. This probably reflected, at least in part, the fact that there was no corporate memory of the way in which the original auxiliary regiment units had functioned (and/or the fact that the AP covering the operations of auxiliary units had not been updated for twenty years). Nevertheless, it was clear that the central theme of the concept of operations was that the auxiliary squadrons should be available at short notice to provide defence of the main base to which they were assigned. The principal variation was in the omission of a support weapons flight, the heaviest weapons actually available at field flight level being the 2-inch mortar and the 66mm LAW. The main deficiency revealed was in the Orderly Room where a staff that was adequate for a regular squadron was being called upon to carry substantial additional burdens, peculiar to the auxiliaries, with respect to organisation, training support, recruiting and public relations. Overall, however, the level of provisioning was outstanding, as was jealously pointed out by TA units when training facilities were shared with them.

The assignment of personnel was a particularly positive aspect, the regular staff associated with the foundation of the auxiliary set-up being hand-picked and first class. Enthusiastic, even by Regiment standards, they were wholly supportive of this rather radical concept (which was not welcomed in every quarter), although on occasion we must have sorely tried their patience by the wide gap in the early days between their innate professionalism and the fumbling of those of us who had no infantry background, not to mention a standard of dress which they could describe only as 'penguin'.

A phrase periodically employed to describe Trenchard's original vision for the Auxiliary Air Force is that he wished to attract those young men who, in an earlier age, would have been attracted to horses and the better sort of yeomanry. Myth makers, as eminent as Len Deighton, have sought to emphasise a dashing image for members of the Auxiliary Air Force. Where did the recruits for these squadrons come from?

A claim may be made that they were different, and it should not be forgotten that in two of the three areas in which the squadrons were seeking to recruit there was a long tradition of Regular Army and TA engagement. The first handful of volunteers included, among the officers at least, two former members of the RAuxAF who had waited twenty years for the force to revive. Two more, one of them from the cavalry, thought that the RAF Regiment would offer them more than their TA formations. And then there was a Peer of the Realm. Amongst the NCOs and airmen were the nursing home owner who could have commuted in his own light aeroplane and a host of professional and well-qualified members of the local, and sometimes quite distant, communities as well as a number of former regulars from the Regiment, the RAF and the Army.

The initial intake soon melded to create an outstanding spirit and a unique way of doing things to further the interests of the squadrons. The auxiliary newspaper correspondent provided excellent PR; county connections produced early visits from Lords Lieutenant, important in gaining local help and acceptance – an (elderly) pilot officer who had first met the AOC at his university might be able to drop a hint if things went astray, and so on. The regulars welcomed the auxiliaries fully into their family with encouragement to join the Regiment clubs and the wider Service clubs and organisations. Typical of the Regiment and of the old-time auxiliaries, there was a lot of socialising on a unit, non-hierarchical, basis adding to essential bonding and creating networking links beyond the Service.

It was not only informally that the new squadrons were able to find different ways of doing things. The squadrons were, for instance, able to introduce women into the RAF Regiment as signallers, the distinction of having sponsored the first going to No 2623 Sqn. Furthermore, with a clearly defined *local* role they were able to develop concepts of operations and tactics designed specifically to meet the needs of the bases they served. These were the subject of seminars at Catterick with spectrum-wide participation from air officers to Flight Commanders.

	Scampton	Lossiemouth	Honington
1980	70%	65%	80%
1981	89%	63%	100%

Fig 1. *Early recruiting performance on the first three RAuxAF Regiment Sqns.*

Participation at the February 1992 event, for instance, included the Deputy CinC Strike Command, Air Mshl Sir Peter Bairstow; AOC 1 Gp, AVM Mike Knight; the Commandant General of the RAF Regiment and the Director of the RAF Regiment and Fire Services plus the Honorary Inspector General and the Inspector of the RAuxAF.

So far as training was concerned, it should be appreciated that the auxiliaries could afford only about a quarter of the time that was available to their regular counterparts. Furthermore, many of the original squadron executives lacked the breadth of professional training appropriate to their functions. To begin with this problem was minimised by specialisation (the establishment of priorities being determined via the kind of Catterick conference to which I have already referred), flexibility in taking advantage of the skills represented on the squadron, and the regular forming and re-forming of cadres to fill gaps. The Depot was generous in finding personnel to visit squadrons for weekends or summer camp to enhance both the quality and the quantity of training that could be fitted in. Auxiliary personnel were welcomed on courses and attachments (sometimes with specially tailored arrangements) with a view to filling gaps in their knowledge. At the County of Lincoln Squadron regular emphasis was given to Methods of Instruction Courses to multiply the training value provided by the more experienced auxiliaries for their newer colleagues. A lot of people worked many more days than the formal requirement, particularly the officers who put in additional weekends to stay 'one jump ahead' and to complete locally the syllabus they would have followed at the Depot on the famous 'J Course'.

Recruiting went well from the outset, the achievements for 1980 and 1981 being reflected at Figure 1. By the end of the pilot period the squadrons were making their presence felt in both operational and ceremonial roles. They were beginning to take part in MINEVALs for their own stations and had built up a reputation for providing a highly proficient 'enemy' which could be employed in the MINEVALs and

TACEVALs of other units. For a hard-pressed Station Commander it was also a great asset to have a resident Regiment squadron available for Service and civic ceremonial. The newcomers were already seen to belong to three families – the auxiliaries, the Regiment and their parent stations.

1982-86

In 1981, before the success of the three pilot squadrons had even been formally evaluated, it was announced in Parliament that there would be an extension of the programme. The next two squadrons, Nos 2624 (County of Oxfordshire) Sqn at Brize Norton and 2625 (County of Cornwall) Sqn at St Mawgan, formed in 1982 and No 2620 (County of Norfolk) Sqn at Marham in 1983.

Of the original three squadrons, No 2503 (County of Lincoln) Sqn, claiming the seniority of its number plate, hosted a function at Scampton in June 1984 to mark the fifth year of the programme. Four months later, consequent upon the phasing out of the V-Force and the planned introduction of the AEW Nimrod, it relocated to RAF Waddington. Flt Lt John Hayton, a founder member of the squadron who had been Deputy CO since 1980, was promoted to squadron leader to take command of the squadron in 1984, making him the first RAuxAF officer to command a Regiment unit for twenty-five years, almost to the day.

During this second phase, as the auxiliary Regiment matured, further consideration was given to the effectiveness of its training methods. One proposal involved the development of a policy, which did not rely entirely on locally delivered training, drawing instead on the Depot's Basic Gunner and Junior Officer courses, supported by a Training and Standards Wing to be based at the Depot. From 1984 squadrons competed for a trophy instituted by Air Cdre Roy Strickland on his retirement as Director of the Regiment. This event was designed to enhance the skill at arms of the squadrons and to do so in such a way as to generate valuable competitive pride while helping to consolidate a sense of unit identity.

At much the same time there was a reappraisal of the equipment needs (probably driven by financial, rather than operational, considerations) under which scales, particularly for vehicles, were reduced. In 1982 the auxiliaries had, for the first time, been asked to provide operational assistance and members of No 2503 Sqn in particular, given the role played by Scampton and Waddington in the Falklands War, volunteered to spend much time, some of it on a full-time basis, in support of their stations.

The future at this time was bright. Not only was there pressure for all main bases to be provided with an auxiliary Regiment squadron, but, under an arrangement with the United States, the RAF Regiment (to a large extent by forming additional RAuxAF squadrons) was also to provide the defence, including SHORAD, of USAF bases in the UK. At Lossiemouth this became manifest in the first trials with auxiliary personnel forming a flight to contribute to the resident RAF Regiment Rapier Squadron.

Waddington was to benefit directly from the Falklands War, because it was there that the RAuxAF Regiment regained an operational air defence capability with the formation in April 1985 of No 2729 (City of Lincoln) Sqn armed with captured Argentinian Oerlikon guns and Skyguard radar. A seized opportunity which had definitely not featured in our long term planning and one which was exploited largely through the efforts of Sqn Ldr Mike Fonfe.

1986 Onwards

It is appropriate to review very briefly the long run out-turn of the re-creation of the RAuxAF Regiment. Despite a major reduction in the size of the RAF Regiment, twenty-three years on, some field squadrons remain whilst others, and some further new squadrons, have taken on the role of Offensive Support Squadrons. The gun squadron and wing which followed No 2729 Sqn and the trials at Lossiemouth led to the establishment of No 27/48 Sqn at Waddington, nominally an RAF Regiment unit but mostly manned by auxiliaries and now counting No 2623 Sqn as an heir. The Training Wing was created, and then became No 2623 Training Squadron when the Depot moved to Honington, although, as I have just pointed out, this unit has undergone a further metamorphosis and is now a sustainment squadron to the Rapier Force.

In the mid-1980s, prior to the passing of the current legislation, auxiliaries began to be substituted for regulars in the performance of certain duties. Operational detachments are now a fact of everyday life and the year 2000 saw the first woman auxiliary member of the Regiment on active service overseas at Ali al Salem.

A group of No 2623 Sqn personnel with an eight-round Rapier fire unit in May 2002.

In 1978 there were just three RAuxAF units which had kept the flag flying for the previous twenty years. They, and the three pilot squadrons which joined them as a project to see whether it was practical to resurrect a Royal Auxiliary Air Force making a widespread contribution to the RAF, have now been joined by, I think – and arrangements seem to change with every gathering I attend – eleven further units, not counting those which have been rebadged from the RAFVR. At a time when the size of the Royal Air Force has shrunk substantially the involvement of new RAuxAF formations has provided the Service with a valuable 'footprint' over much of the country. Twenty years on, concepts and needs have changed but the formation of the three field squadrons in 1979 had clearly been a pivotal point in the development of reserves for the Royal Air Force.

MEDICS AND MOVERS IN THE GULF WAR

Squadron Leader Jon Pote

There have been two very contrasting aspects to Sqn Ldr Jon Pote's medical career. On the one hand, having qualified as a doctor in 1972, and following a stint with the Flying Doctor Service in Australia, he became a country GP in Devonshire in 1979. On the other, he has been on call with No 22 Sqn since 1980, and he still is; at the last count he had been involved in no fewer than 154 Search and Rescue incidents. Furthermore, he has been serving with No 4626 (Aeromedical Evacuation) Sqn of the RAuxAF since 1988, and he still is.

Introduction

A total of 252 members of the Royal Auxiliary Air Force and thirty-four members of the RAFVR or RAFRO served in support of Operation GRANBY. The units involved were Nos 7006 (Intelligence) and 7644 (Public Relations) Flights of the RAFVR, and Nos 4624 (Movements) and 4626 (Aeromedical Evacuation) Squadrons of the RAuxAF.

Squadron History

No 4626 (County of Wiltshire) Sqn, RAuxAF, was formed alongside RAF Hospital, Wroughton, on 9 September 1983, one of several units formed as a result of the Falkland conflict. It moved to Hullavington in April 1986, and to Lyneham in May 1993. It is tasked with supplementing regular aeromedical evacuation assets in time of conflict, and with supporting them in peacetime operations, by providing for the reception, treatment and escorting of casualties from the combat zone to appropriate hospital facilities. This involves two distinct tasks: providing holding facilities at an airhead, and escorting casualties in flight.

Members have flown some five million miles on duty in war and peace, and recently served for in excess of 1000 days in support of Exercise SAIF SAREEA II, providing the bulk of the aeromedical personnel during the peak six weeks, which generated one of the largest peacetime 'lifts' in history.

Background to the Gulf War

On 2 August 1990, Iraq invaded Kuwait 'to reclaim its 17th Province'. There was immediate international condemnation, but on 8 August Iraq formally annexed Kuwait. On 11 August the UK deployed Jaguars and Tornados to the area, and on the 22nd the USA announced a large call-out of its reservists. Squadron members took a great interest in these developments. Interestingly, our Annual Continuous Training (ACT) in 1989 had been in Cyprus, and in 1990 it was delayed as RAF Germany, our intended host, was at a higher state of readiness due to the Iraqi invasion. The unit finally deployed to RAF Halton in November, to practice for the first time operating under Collective Protection ('Colpro') measures in an NBC environment. Whilst we were there, Saudi Arabia increased its readiness state (8 November), and the British Army deployed its 1st Armoured Division for service in the desert (22 November). Members expected to stay in uniform after ACT ended, as Iraq had been given an ultimatum to withdraw from Kuwait by 15 January 1991 or face the consequences, but in the event they went home to prepare for the inevitable.

Just before Christmas, all personnel gathered at our HQ to be addressed by AVM John Harris, Assistant Chief of Defence Staff (Personnel and Logistics), who was fresh from a meeting with the Secretary of State for Defence, Tom King. Also on the podium were AVM Alan Johnson (PMO Strike Command), Michael Stewart (Head of S10(Air)) and the Inspector of the Royal Auxiliary Air Force, Gp Capt Mike Tinley. Our Honorary Air Commodore, AVM Riseley Prichard, and our CO, Wg Cdr Eley, sat with squadron members. The ACDS exhorted us to volunteer *en masse*, the calling out of reservists being politically controversial. Various issues, such as security of employment, our families, life insurance and pay were discussed without much progress being made and the meeting was in danger of achieving nothing. Finally, a junior member of the unit settled the matter: he asked the air marshal if it might be more useful not to ask us to volunteer, but rather to ask how many would apply for exemption if the Queen's Order were to be invoked and the squadron ordered to the Gulf. A clearly discomfited man, he asked the question. Not a single hand rose. That ended the meeting and the unit was formally called-up a few days later.

Call-up, training and deployment

Of some 140 auxiliary personnel who were called up, only six considered themselves unavailable for service. An Exemption Board heard their submissions, and all six agreed to leave the RAuxAF. The rest were embodied within the Royal Air Force. Six more were medically unfit to deploy overseas; they trained with fellow members and were then seconded to the RAF Hospital at Wroughton. Thus were the concerns of senior officers (and the Friday night jibes of some ill-informed regulars) laid to rest: 96% of the unit became effective, and 92% deployed to the war zone, figures any regular unit would be proud of. They were augmented by a similar number of RAF Musicians to act as stretcher-bearers, an entirely new role for them.

Training now had a new focus. For the first time we received firearms training while NBC training and the Geneva Convention took on a new interest. Multiple inoculations, later to cause great controversy, were received. Life became very serious, but the 'auxiliary spirit' shone through: When officers were ordered to remove the brass 'A's from their shoulder braid, they refused, preferring instead to paint them black 'for tactical considerations', just as officers of the 'Twenty-One Squadrons' are said to have done in 1939.

A small advance party under Sqn Ldr Dixon flew to Al Jubayl on the north-east coast of Saudi Arabia, the rest, led by myself, following on 14 January. Forty-five personal weapons were collected from the armoury at Brize Norton and everyone travelled on a Kuwaiti Airlines Boeing 747 with respirator and NBC suit to hand. It was dark, and pouring with rain, as tired personnel deplaned at Al Jubayl, still with many hours to go before their exhausted bodies finally lay in uncomfortable tents at Baldrick Lines, the reception camp. This was a matter of mere hours before the UN's deadline to Iraq expired. Thirty-six hours later, the flights had dispersed to their operational locations:

a. A Flight went to King Khalid International Airport at Riyadh, where they were collocated with 205(V) General Surgical Hospital.

b. B Flight remained at Al Jubayl to work with 33 General Surgical Hospital.

c. The half-strength C-1 Flight went to Bahrein, to work with No 1 RAF War Hospital.

d. The similarly depleted C-2 Flight went to King Abdul Aziz RSAF Base at Dhahran, to work with Mobile Surgical Troop Alpha.

In each case, the auxiliaries took over facilities already set-up by regulars from No 1 Aeromedical Evacuation Squadron, who then moved to Al Qaysumah, the forward operating base near the Iraq/Kuwait/Saudi Arabia tri-border point whence we would later collect the bulk of the casualties.

A Hercules offloading six stretcher cases and one walker at Riyadh,
28 February 1991.

Both Riyadh and Al Jubayl were nodes in the evacuation chain, receiving casualties from Al Qaysumah and outloading them to Akrotiri and the UK. Any held for more than a few hours were stabilised and cared for in the partner army hospitals until they were fit to fly, and an aircraft was available. In general, B Flight handled the bulk of the casualties until the ground offensive started in February and the numbers rose. Thereafter, the Hercules, bearing only a tiny red cross by the crew door (which actually marked the position of the first-aid kit!) in deference to the fact that they hauled troops and munitions on the outward leg, flew a triangular route from Riyadh to Al Qaysumah (where the in-flight teams re-roled the aircraft to accept stretchers), on to Al Jubayl, where neurological, ophthalmic and burns cases were deplaned for 33 General Surgical Hospital, and back to Riyadh with the remainder.

Neither C-1 nor C-2 Flights were in the evacuation chain, seemingly located purely as a local resource to support the substantial RAF detachments they adjoined. Both relinquished about half of their personnel to Riyadh and Al Jubayl respectively once the ground war started.

Thereafter, auxiliary personnel provided air escort teams of four, consisting of flight-nursing officers, flight nurses and flight-nursing attendants (usually with a supernumerary medical officer) for the frequent Hercules sorties, and ground-handling teams at the four locations. They also occasionally escorted casualties in both American and British helicopters. Regular RAF personnel escorted all routine strategic aeromedical flights to the UK and Cyprus, although some high-dependency patients were escorted home by auxiliaries on special flights. Thus the auxiliaries did not simply augment their regular counterparts, but were the backbone of the vital intra-theatre sector of the evacuation chain. Additional duties included armed guarding, providing drivers for other operational units, public health and lecturing on the medical aspects of NBC warfare.

At the end of the conflict, despite many personnel volunteering to work in Iraq with the Kurds and Marsh Arabs (eventually four did go to Kurdistan with a charity), the unit was one of the first to return to the UK, arriving on 10 March to be met and thanked in person by the Secretary of State, Tom King. Politics were once again in the ascendant, however, and everyone was demobilised from regular service (with three weeks disembarkation leave) that same day.

A Flight, Headquarters and the Air Escort Teams

A Flight, the Squadron HQ, and the air escort teams were collocated at King Khalid Airport, Riyadh. A Flight had a quiet time until the ground war started. Of all the flights, they were the most integrated with a hospital, acting as the evacuation unit for 205(V) General Surgical Hospital, a Glasgow-based TA unit which occupied the bulk of an unfinished underground airport terminal building. With only six stretcher patients during January, the time was put to good use preparing for February, when seventy-five stretcher and fifty-nine ambulant casualties were escorted to Riyadh, taken into 205(V) GSH, and eventually outloaded onto VC10s bound for the UK. Reaching the cargo door of a VC10, many metres above ground level, without the customary ground support equipment proved to be a challenge. Some of those with airline backgrounds experimented with luggage elevators and found that a stretcher, laid on the endless inclined belt, stood a good chance of reaching the top with the patient unscathed, whereupon a pair of agile medical assistants could grab it just before disaster became inevitable. There were no mishaps with our 'live luggage'.

A Flight provided all the constituted air escort teams, seven in all, usually accompanied by a medical officer, of whom six were available after Major Tan, of the Singapore Air Force, joined the flight. The triangular route took just under four hours: a relaxed outward stage, seated on cargo, to Al Qaysumah where the aircraft were re-roled to accept the casualties from No 1 Aeromedical Evacuation Squadron; a second leg to Al Jubayl, where some were off-loaded; and then back to Riyadh with the remainder. Necessary medical care in the air was fortunately not too challenging, even though some patients were emplaned whilst still recovering consciousness after emergency surgery.

What might have been is shown by the day's orders for 25 February. The first of sixteen Hercules was due to leave Riyadh at 0345 hrs, the last at 0145 the next morning, each escort team completing three round-trips, twelve hours airborne plus six hours of on/off-loading during the 24-hour cycle. Up to 1000 casualties per day, possibly NBC contaminated, were expected, sixty per aircraft, this unimaginable horror lasting for the five days that the ground forces could remain in all-out action. In the event, every few days, just a few casualties appeared, often outnumbered by their escorts. The miracle that all had not even dared to hope for had occurred.

B Flight

B Flight remained at Al Jubayl, taking over the Aeromedical Staging Facility (ASF) there. As their partner unit, 33 General Surgical Hospital, RAMC, was 30 miles away, they had to function as an autonomous patient-holding facility, with the ability to care for, feed and guard patients for up to 24 hours unaided. It was by far the largest ASF in the evacuation chain, expanding to seven wards capable of holding 100 stretcher cases and 120 ambulant ones, as well as a resuscitation bay for up to six unstable casualties. It is in the nature of the wounds suffered on the battlefield and the need to do the greatest good for the greatest number that surgery close to the battlefront is restricted to life- and limb-saving procedures, resulting in some casualties arriving further down the chain in need of further urgent care.

The bulk of the 848 casualties of the war, over 90% of whom were non-battle injuries and illnesses, had passed through Al Jubayl and then directly to the UK via VC10 *before* the ground war started.

B Flight can also claim to be the engineering flight of No 4626 (AE) Sqn: Undeterred by the fact that their Royal Engineer-built underground air raid shelter proved *not* to be impervious to an American bulldozer carelessly driven over it, luckily when unoccupied, B Flt's personnel promptly made good the damage. That done, they went on to construct a metal apron one hundred metres square between the ASF and the nearby

B Flight's Aeromedical Staging Facility at Al Jubayl flying the regionally appropriate Red Crescent.

runway, allowing aircraft to off-load patients directly into the facility rather than using the distant, and congested, aircraft parking area.

During the ground war, a number of wounded Iraqi prisoners passed through the facility and, after the main fighting was over, B Flt, uniquely, sent several teams into Kuwait City to recover casualties.

C-1 Flight

C-1 Flight drove to Bahrein, via the spectacular causeway, where it assumed responsibility for a twenty-or-so bedded ward in a prefabricated structure. Being collocated with No 1 RAF War Hospital, the former RAF Hospital, Ely (which was to disband *in situ* at the war's end) they would have held patients only briefly, with the option of returning those who deteriorated to the excellent care of that hospital, or to the nearby Battleshock Rehabilitation Unit for those with post traumatic stress problems. In the event, few, if any, casualties passed their way.

Interestingly, from an historical perspective, Muharraq airfield, where C-1 Flight trained, was the Forward Operating Base for the Buccaneers of No 12 Sqn. In 1943, No 626 Sqn had been formed from C Flight of 12 Sqn at Wickenby, Lincolnshire, whence it operated Lancasters. The members of the No 626 Sqn Association took a close interest in the activities of No 4626 Sqn in the Gulf.

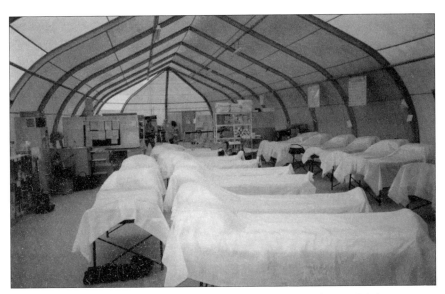

'The miracle'; the empty beds at C-1 Flight's facility at Muharraq.

C-2 Flight

C-2 Flight arrived at Dhahran late at night. After just one hour in bed, everyone was woken by members of the RAF Regiment hammering on the portacabin walls and shouting 'Red! Red! Air Attack Red!' The war had started. Respirators and NBC clothing were donned for real for the first time and, whilst it was later found that the stand-to was merely a precaution, because the Tornados were heading into Iraq on their first raids, the effect on everyone had been profound. For the next few days everybody slept in the Aeromedical Staging Facility on the airfield, both to be immediately available, should there be casualties in the RAF Detachment, and also to be protected by the Patriot batteries.

Next day, regular personnel from No 1 Aeromedical Evacuation Squadron moved out towards Al Qaysumah after a rapid handover, leaving the auxiliaries in charge of a tented facility with a dozen beds, surrounded by a palisade of concrete-filled drums (which had formerly held tomato puree!) piled three metres high. The Royal Engineers had also constructed an above-ground air-raid shelter of drums, steel plate and sandbags, said to be proof against a near miss by a 500 lb warhead. This shelter was to be their sleeping accommodation for the first week.

On the second night, just after a Scud alert had been terminated, a group standing outside was surprised by an apparent explosion nearby. This rapidly revealed itself to be a Patriot anti-missile missile launching. Transfixed, they watched it soar vertically upwards, followed by a huge flash above the clouds. The first Scud had been destroyed, three miles above them, making history. For the first time since WW II, an auxiliary unit was on active service *and* under enemy fire.

Life in Dhahran settled into a routine after that. A convenient site beside a taxiway for the loading of patients was agreed with our Saudi hosts (after many cups of coffee) and vehicles suitable to move loaded stretchers were identified amongst the resources of the RAF Detachment. Training continued, but the expected flood of casualties never materialised. A few aeromedical transfers were made, the first, a colonel injured in a road traffic accident, being flown to 33 General Surgical Hospital at Al Jubayl in a US Army UH-1E Huey, 'Dust-Off 490', of the 348th Medical Detachment, appropriately enough a Reserve unit activated for duty in the Gulf. A further sortie was flown in a UH-60 Black Hawk, SAC Elford escorting the patient, but essentially the detachment trained – and counted Scuds, silhouettes of over twenty eventually being stencilled on the Land Rover's door. Any complacency was ill-founded, however, as was demonstrated towards the end of the campaign. During a meal at their accommodation, a huge explosion brought down parts of the roof onto the table. There were no injuries to squadron personnel, but a few hundred yards away twenty newly-arrived American reservists died as a Scud hit their accommodation – the worst Allied disaster of the war.

Lessons Learned

No 4626 Sqn learned many lessons during the Gulf War, both as individuals and as a unit. Perhaps the most important lesson for the individual was that a call-out for active service was a real possibility. It had never before seemed possible, short of war with Russia. Individuals, of whom some twenty are still with the unit today, learned how to operate an Aeromedical Staging Facility overseas, and wrote the first British SOPs for such facilities. Equally, and very importantly, the RAF learned that auxiliaries, although perhaps somewhat bemused, *would* rally to the cause without exception. It therefore followed that auxiliaries were worth whatever input of equipment and training the Big Air Force could give them, the result being an officer or airman as good as most regulars, better than many, and at just over a tenth of the cost in peacetime. Important lessons were also learned about recruitment, notably the need to attract personnel with relevant skills, not *just* nurses and doctors, for example, but nurses and doctors experienced in acute trauma.

Recruitment has also become more focused, candidates recognising that active service is a distinct possibility. Furthermore, the squadron now has equipment officially held on its charge, rather than being begged or borrowed. Nevertheless, there are still improvements to be made, especially the need to provide auxiliaries with equipment and training that is fully comparable with that given to their regular counterparts. Should that ever occur, the auxiliary will be a truly capable animal.

Acknowledgements
The author wishes to acknowledge the assistance he received while preparing his paper from AVM R A Riseley Prichard, the Honorary Air Commodore of No 4626 (AE) Sqn at the time, and from various contemporary members of the unit, including its erstwhile CO, Wg Cdr A G Eley, and Sqn Ldr (now Wg Cdr) T E Martin (OC B Flt, Al Jubayl).

No 4624 SQN'S EXPERIENCE
(contributed by Sqn Ldr Tony Freeman)

Members of No 4624 (County of Oxford) Movements Squadron at Brize Norton had a different kind of war. They were not asked to 'volunteer' until the offensive started on 17 January. By this time, the men and materiel necessary for such a campaign were already in place, the regular Supply and Movements organisation having performed miracles at the expense of long hours and very little leave. The arrival of the auxiliary 'movers' permitted additional shifts of manpower to be introduced, which gave the regulars some respite. It also created scope for 'back filling', releasing manpower for overseas, whilst also providing a pool of manpower for deployment in the event of casualties and to assist with any prolonged periods of re-supply. In the event, this proved unnecessary.

Unlike the aeromedical personnel, many of whom undertook aeromedical evacuation in peacetime or could utilise their civilian skills, most 'movers' required a period of time to work up to operational efficiency. Whilst it is true that auxiliaries are trained to the same standards as their regular counterparts, there is no substitute for hands-on experience and it took three or four weeks of practical experience for most personnel to achieve a satisfactory level of operational competence.

Some 130 'movers' were deployed. Detachments of about fifty personnel were sent to man the Cargo Section at Brize Norton and the Traffic Section at Lyneham. Additionally, a small UK MAMS team was deployed to Wildenrath in Germany, whence much of the RAF's effort was mounted. Other personnel provided support at HQ Strike Command and at the railheads serving the trooping flights from the UK. All auxiliary movements personnel had been demobilised by April.

Pay and administrative shortcomings manifested themselves as a result of there being no procedures in place to cope with the unexpected numbers of reservists, for whom there was no legal mechanism for call out short of General War. Many of these issues have since been addressed with new legislation, but it says much for the patience and forbearance of both regulars and reservists during Operation GRANBY that significant numbers of the Royal Air Force's reserves were utilised in such an effective fashion.

AFTERNOON DISCUSSION PERIOD

Gp Capt Jock Heron. Could I ask about the assumption that Vampire pilots couldn't possibly fly Hunters from time to time at weekends. For those of us who trained in the mid-to-late-1950s and transitioned from the Vampire to the Hunter with something like 250 hours total, it does seem a very conservative attitude.

Air Cdre Ian Atkinson. I do not think that there was any doubt among the pilots that, given the training opportunities, they would have been perfectly able to cope. That said, it would have been nice to have had an interim aeroplane. But the Hunter programme rather assumed that the squadrons were going to be able to continue to function. So far as No 613 Sqn was concerned, we were happy at Ringway but the civil side was getting busier and one could see that a time would come when it would no longer be practical to operate fighters alongside commercial traffic. Nevertheless, we would have welcomed the chance to fly Hunters.

Jefford. I don't think that anyone ever seriously suggested that an auxiliary pilot would be *unable* to cope with the Hunter. The problem was how to provide him with one. The piece of paper I have in my hand is a copy of the statement which was drafted for the Secretary of State when he was preparing to announce to the House that the auxiliary squadrons were to be shut down. One of the several reasons cited was that it had proved impossible, that is to say impractical, to train many auxiliary pilots on Hunters. The original idea of having six Hunter pilots per squadron had soon been cut to two and even then little real progress had been made, because introducing the Hunter into service had been a fairly protracted affair (remember the problems with gun-firing?) and priority simply had to be given to the regulars. (*See also pages 144-154. Ed*)

Wg Cdr Colin Cummings. In the context of reserves and auxiliaries, where did the Air Transport Auxiliary fit in?

Jefford. We had hoped to find a slot for the ATA but the programme was overfull as it was, so we had to abandon the idea, taking refuge in the fact that they were not really a military organisation. They were, in a fairly remote sense, in that they came under the Department of Civil Aviation which, in turn, came under the Air Ministry. But that is as far as it went and, in essence, the ATA was a civilian organisation, perhaps 'paramilitary' would be an even better description.

The pilots tended to suffer from some limitation which precluded their being able to fly with the military, often a medical condition, but more commonly simply age and/or sex. The ATA was initially fostered by British Airways/BOAC, rather than the RAF, although CFS offered early single-to-twin conversion courses until the ATA set up its own school at White Waltham. The core functions of the ATA were to collect aeroplanes from the factory and deliver them to RAF storage units or from storage to a user. The central tasking cell was at Andover where it was collocated with HQ 41 Gp, the formation responsible for the storage and movement of all RAF aircraft, although I would imagine that the Ministry of Aircraft Production would have had some influence over operations.

Arthur Spencer. One of Jeff's slides indicated that in September 1948 there were ninety-eight navigators on the strength of the VR. I was one of them and I had already undertaken my first fortnight's annual training by then. In 1949 a few of us were given the opportunity to fly on the Berlin Airlift. We assembled at Oakington, sixteen strong, whence we were flown to Lübeck to spend a couple of weeks flying the corridors into and out of Gatow. It was a very interesting experience and I think that there were plans to repeat the exercise. In the event, however, the airlift began to run down and I think that we were the only group to go.

I continued to fly with No 14 RFS at Hamble until it closed down in 1953, although I managed to squeeze in one more summer camp at Redhill which stayed open for another year. There was no more flying for the VR after that but we were still there for a while. I was given a war appointment at HQ Transport Command which meant that I was issued with a railway warrant which would get me to Upavon in case the balloon ever went up.

Alan Pollock. I would just like to add something to what Lord Monro said this morning. The contribution of the AAF went beyond mere tallies of scores. Take Sqn Ldr Ronald Kellett, for instance, a long-service AAF officer, he helped to set up No 249 Sqn, which would later become the top-scoring RAF fighter squadron of WW II, before repeating the exercise with No 303 (Polish) Sqn. He subsequently commanded No 96 Sqn before becoming Wing Leader at North Weald, ending the war with five confirmed victories, a DSO and a DFC after which he rejoined the RAuxAF to command No 615 Sqn until 1949. I just wanted to make the point that the AAF was about individuals as well as squadrons.

No 615 Sqn's identity was kept alive in 1945 by grafting its number plate onto the erstwhile No 135 Sqn, but it is doubtful whether many (any?) AAF personnel will have been on strength at this stage.

Air Cdre Graham Pitchfork. Echoing Sir John Barraclough's earlier observation on the wider wartime achievements of the AAF, it is often forgotten that that the first RAF squadron to be equipped with jets was an auxiliary unit, No 616 (South Yorkshire) Sqn, although, as Jeff has pointed out, there would have been relatively few AAF personnel still on strength by 1944. Nevertheless, OC 616 Sqn, Wg Cdr Andrew McDowell, had established a fine combat record flying with an AAF unit, No 602 Sqn, during the Battle of Britain.

Sir Frederick Sowrey. Could I make a couple of points. First, although it has been made clear that there were very few AAF pilots still flying with AAF squadrons by 1942, many of the groundcrew were still on strength. It is, I suggest, the groundcrew who provide the cement which holds a squadron together. In the case of the unit that I would eventually command in the early 1950s, No 615 Sqn, our AAF airmen stayed together through the Battle of Britain and later they all went out to the Far East. It is true that their numbers were being steadily depleted but there was always a hard core. In my experience, it is the groundcrew who *make* a squadron; if your airmen are behind you, you can be confident that your squadron will succeed. As an example, of 'mucking in', I well recall my first stint with No 615 Sqn in 1946; the first order of business was to whitewash the Nissen hut that was to be the squadron's HQ. It was two-man job, because there were only two of us, a lone corporal, who was the first airmen to sign up, and myself, the Training Officer.

The second point I would like to make is to acknowledge the advantages that were to be gained from being stationed on an RAF, as distinct from a civilian, airfield. As OC 615 Sqn at Biggin Hill in the 1950s I was always able to make a direct comparison between my own unit's performance and that of the regulars. As, I think, Ian Atkinson suggested, I would say that, at that time, a good RAuxAF squadron probably achieved standards similar to those of a middle-rank regular unit.

One last comment. While our Vampires and Meteors were getting a little long in the tooth by the mid-1950s, they were perfectly capable of countering the Tu-4, which was still reckoned to be a threat at the time. Furthermore, we were able to demonstrate this because we always participated in Fighter Command exercises. We could not expect everyone to turn out mid-week, of course, but we could usually field four Meteors with competent pilots (and I had some very good ones, Hugh Merryweather and 'Pee Wee' Judge, for instance, and I had taken over from one Neville Duke). With chaps of that calibre we could put on a good show and I am sure that we impressed the crews of the 'enemy' Washingtons when they were confronted by a Meteor doing a head-on attack at a great rate of knots. You had to trim it very tail heavy, so that you were pushing hard, which meant that you could just let go of the stick at the last possible moment and still clear the bomber adequately.

Up to that point, I think that the post-war RAuxAF squadrons had been making a positive and realistic contribution to national defence. As we have seen, however, it would have been very difficult to keep doing this into the 1960s and beyond.

Paul Sargent. Prior to the establishment of the Air Training Corps in 1941 I was a cadet in the Air Defence Cadet Corps. Does anyone know when that corps came into being and what category of officers manned it? It was run very differently from the ATC. I recall, for instance, that we had to buy our own uniforms; you could either pay sixpence a week or a lump sum of fifteen shillings. Can anyone help me?

Jefford. I can answer that one, but I do not have the details with me today. Perhaps I could include a note in the published proceedings.

The note is as follows: The Air Defence Cadet Corps (ADCC) was another enterprise which owed its existence to the energetic Air Cdre

John Chamier during his tenure as Secretary-General of the Air League of the British Empire. The first ADCC unit formed at Leicester in July 1938. MRAF Sir John Salmond agreed to be the Chairman of the organisation and later that year he inspected No 2 (Watford) Sqn. There were a total of thirty-seven squadrons by the end of the year and another hundred or so had been formed before the outbreak of war. A degree of recognition by the Air Ministry brought a modicum of financial support (3/6d per head) but the bulk of the administrative costs were underwritten by the Air League. At the coal face, the financial burden fell squarely upon the shoulders of the membership. Accommodation and facilities were provided through sponsorship and fund-raising organised by the local committees that were formed to run the squadrons in accordance with a set of rules devised by the Air League. The League also published a training syllabus but this was not rigidly adhered to and there were no examinations. Officers were given 'Air League commissions' which attracted neither a salary nor expenses. Officers and cadets alike were obliged to buy their own uniforms. Despite these practical handicaps, enthusiasm was such that some 200 squadrons came into being.

In December 1939 the Air Ministry began a review of the existing facilities for pre-entry training. This eventually led, among other things, to the establishment of the Air Training Corps. The ATC project was approved by the War Cabinet in December 1940 and its formation was formally authorised by the Royal Warrant of 4 February 1941 to which Wg Cdr Margiotta referred in his paper on the UASs. The foundations of the ATC were provided by the pre-existing ADCC units, most (all?) of which were absorbed into the new organisation, being allocated the first 200 squadron numbers. As an additional mark of distinction, the first ATC unit to have been formed in each region/county was permitted to add the suffix 'F' (for Founder) after its number. Many of the ADCC's officers were also retained, usually via membership of the RAFVR.

CHAIRMAN'S CLOSING REMARKS

Allow me, if I may, to make one or two remarks in drawing matters to a close. I think you will all agree that we have had a most interesting day. We have covered a great deal of ground and opened up new lines of thought which, had we had more time, would have been well worth exploring in even greater depth.

We have examined how and why the RAF's various reserve forces came into being, what use has been made of them and how valuable they have been. We have seen how Lord Trenchard's vision of part-time volunteer reservists forming part of the front-line actually came to fruition in the Battle of Britain in particular, and even earlier in the Battle of France. We have also considered the ways in which the Service exercised both imagination and pragmatism in the exploitation of its reserves, especially during and after WW II. Finally, we have heard that, despite the virtual dismemberment of the Royal Auxiliary Air Force in 1957, the Trenchard mould was not broken beyond repair. Its ethos was maintained by a handful of small maritime units and, in the presentations on the roles of just two of today's squadrons, we have learned something of the renaissance that the RAuxAF has undergone since 1979.

I think that it would be appropriate for me, in my capacity as Honorary Inspector General, to claim a moment or two to say a few words about today's force. Happily, the constraints that were built into the succession of whiskery old Reserve Forces Acts were discarded in 1996, and the new legislation, in which some of us in this room played a part in drafting, allows much greater flexibility to both the Government and Commanders in their use of reserve forces. It certainly permits much greater flexibility than before and, leaving aside the embodiment of auxiliary personnel in war, they may now, when necessary, be employed in response to a peacetime crisis and they can even be found participating in routine day-to-day Service activities. Another important step taken at much the same time was the amalgamation of the RAuxAF with the war appointable elements of the RAFVR; it has proved to be a happy marriage.

Today we have heard something of the work of the current RAuxAF Regiment, aeromedical and movement squadrons but we can also field air-transportable surgical, operations support, intelligence, photographic interpretation, public relations and police squadrons, all roles which contribute directly to supporting the front-line capability of the Royal Air Force. There are currently nineteen such units, the newest of which actually began recruiting as recently as this week.

In addition to these ground-based units, Lyneham has a flight of forty-five aircrew operating the Hercules. In all there are more than 100 auxiliary aircrew who still fly with the RAF, all of them ex-regulars who have completed their engagements but who wish to continue to make a contribution. This arrangement is very different from the RAuxAF squadrons of yesteryear but the RAF is very different too. Rather than deploying formed units, as we would have done in the past, the aim today is to assemble a tailor-made force appropriate to the occasion by drawing on a pool of specialists trained in a wide variety of roles. Since auxiliary personnel can be made available in support of RAF operations anywhere in the world as individuals, sections, flights or squadrons, they are ideally suited to the support of this concept. In recent years our people have served with distinction in Afghanistan, Pakistan, Sierra Leone, Turkey, the Falklands, Cyprus, Saudi Arabia, Oman and in various NATO countries, as well as in the UK.

The roles of the modern RAuxAF maybe be very different, but they are just as demanding of part-time volunteers as ever. There is no question that the professional skill, enthusiasm and spirit demonstrated by today's men and women are the equal of those displayed by their pre-war forerunners. They are inspired by the courage and achievements of their predecessors, and are proud of the invaluable contribution that they know that they themselves are making to the capabilities of today's RAF. Most of today's auxiliary personnel have 'day jobs' and family commitments, which means that each one of them is, in Winston Churchill's words 'twice a citizen'.

Ladies and Gentlemen, it remains only for me, on behalf of us all, to thank AVM Nigel Baldwin and his committee, and particularly Jeff Jefford and Tony Freeman, for their sterling work in planning and arranging today's seminar. Our speakers, I am sure you will agree, have been exceptional. I congratulate them all and thank them all for presenting us with so much interesting information, for stimulating such an interesting discussion and for a thoroughly enjoyable day.

THE DEMISE OF THE AUXILIARY FIGHTER SQUADRONS REVISITED

by the Editor

Because the afternoon question period was running late, Gp Capt Peter Harris forbore to prolong the proceedings by raising another issue from the floor, but he did subsequently write to offer the following observations as a contribution to the discussion:

'The Air Ministry view in the mid-1950s, that auxiliary pilots could not be trained to fly second-generation jets to an acceptable standard, still prevailed at the MOD when I was Inspector RAuxAF thirty years later. However, even in the mid-1980s the US Air Force Reserve (AFRes) and the US Air National Guard (ANG) were doing just that, not only using ex-regular pilots but also training others from scratch. Indeed, the air defence of the Panama Canal Zone at that time was provided solely by AFRes/ANG squadrons operating on a *roulement* basis for two to four weeks at a time; furthermore, many Military Airlift Command transport aircraft were operated by the ANG, several of them winning international competitions against strong RAF and other foreign entries. I wonder, therefore, whether the policy was dictated not so much by a perceived, but not proven, training capability so much as by Treasury constraints, and a preference to concentrate the limited resources available on a smaller but all-regular force.'

Although the afternoon presentations did address some of the factors which led to the disbandment of the RAuxAF as a flying organisation, the constraints imposed by time precluded their being explored in much depth. Furthermore, for reasons that will become clear, the contemporary public debate over the demise of the RAuxAF had actually been conducted on a relatively superficial level. Gp Capt Harris's note suggests that there may still be some uncertainty over the real rationale behind the disbandment decision of 1956 so, at the risk of a degree of repetition, it is perhaps worth examining the circumstances in a little more detail, especially as it may be considered that several of these arguments would still have been valid in the 1980s and even today.

The first point to make is that no one, at least no one in a position of authority, ever seriously suggested that auxiliary pilots would be *unable* to cope with swept-wing aeroplanes. After all, the typical auxiliary pilot of the mid-1950s had been recently trained by the RAF (or the RCAF) to exactly the same standard as his regular counterpart. Since a first-tourist regular could fly a Hunter, it was axiomatic that an auxiliary would be equally capable of doing so. While the RAF did have some reservations over the effectiveness of part-time pilots, it is clear that these reservations were not, could not have been, to do with their competence. There were certainly grounds for concern but these were rooted in the Service's inability to provide the auxiliaries with a worthwhile degree of access to state-of-the-art aeroplanes. In practical terms, of course, this amounted to the same thing in the end.

That aside, Peter Harris surmises that the real reason behind the demise of the squadrons may have been funding. To a degree, he is quite right, but there is no need for speculation over this issue, because George Ward made no bones about it in his statement to the House on 23 January 1957. As *Hansard* records, he said: 'With the resources available to us it is not possible either to re-equip the squadrons with Hunters or to retain them any longer in their existing role except at the expense of regular units.' In short, we could not afford the auxiliaries and, at the time, that was the only reason for their disbandment cited by the Secretary of State.

Although Ward had plumped for cost and left it that, it had not been the only factor influencing the disbandment decision. The draft statement that had been prepared for him had actually offered a number of arguments and, although Ward elected not to deploy them, they are perhaps worth examining here. First of all, as Tony Freeman noted, there had been an attempt to give some auxiliary pilots swept-wing experience by fostering arrangements made with regular squadrons. Despite reducing the number of nominated auxiliary pilots from six per squadron to just two, however, little real progress had been made with this scheme. This was partly because of teething problems with the early Hunters, which meant that there were barely enough flying hours to go around for the regulars, let alone trying to keep the auxiliaries up to scratch.

But there were other problems with this arrangement. It would have been relatively straightforward for a couple of pilots of, say, No 600 Sqn to stroll across to the offices of the collocated No 41 Sqn in the hope of begging a trip in a Hunter at Biggin Hill, but how easy was this going to be for pilots based at Abbotsinch, Hooton Park, Llandow, Filton and elsewhere? The regular fighter squadrons were stationed in the south and east, which was on the 'wrong' side of the island for many auxiliaries (indeed the wrong island altogether for the pilots of Aldergrove's No 502 Sqn) and there was no guarantee that, having commuted across the Pennines, a Hunter would actually be available, especially over the weekend.

Another factor which George Ward did mention, but which he made no attempt to amplify, was the 'existing role' of the auxiliaries. What he had in mind was the rapidly evolving threat. Although the squadrons had been reprieved in 1955 by assigning them the task of countering an airborne assault, it is legitimate to ask whether such a commitment had ever been a realistic one. This hare may have been started as early as 1951 when, during the Commons debate on that year's Defence White Paper, Anthony Eden had suggested that, by using between 500 and 1000 four-engined aeroplanes, the Russians might be able to air drop six divisions of troops on the UK. In point of fact, the Russians never had a transport force of anything like that size, of course, so the anti-invasion task had always involved a somewhat Quixotic scenario. The other role that had been considered for the auxiliaries in 1955, that of continuing to counter the Tu-4, had also been clutching at straws, because Tupolev's equivalent to the Valiant, the Tu-16 *Badger*, was already operational with the Soviet Air Force by then.

While the advent of high performance jet bombers capable of delivering nuclear weapons from high altitude had plainly rendered the Meteor and Vampire obsolete, they had also raised increasingly pressing concerns over the availability, or readiness, of the defences. As Tony Freeman put it, 'it was by now universally accepted (except perhaps at squadron level) that, *in practical terms*, part-time pilots could not be trained on swept-wing aircraft so as to be *immediately* available in war.' Again, it was not suggested that auxiliary pilots were *incapable* of flying Hunters but it was doubted that they could maintain an adequate degree of currency *and* be able to react quickly enough if/when the balloon went up. This was another of the arguments that had been offered to Ward but one which he also chose not to deploy.

This is not to deny that the 'establishment' of the regular air force harboured reservations over the real, as distinct from the potential, capabilities of its part-time units. It did, and it always had done. But these concerns were not without foundation; they were based on past experience and a realistic appreciation of current performance. For instance, as long ago as July 1939, Sir Hugh Dowding wrote:

'I calculate that by January 1940 I shall have 25 Regular Squadrons equipped with modern types plus 14 Auxiliary Squadrons in various stages of efficiency. Of these 14, 6 will be nearly as efficient as Regulars, 5 will be semi-efficient, and the remainder of little value.'

It is clear that this situation had not escaped the attention of the then Director of Plans. Twelve years later, by then CAS, Sir John Slessor wrote in a note to Hoyt Vandenberg, his opposite number at the Pentagon:

'Unlike when the Auxiliary Squadrons first started, twenty years ago, you cannot train the amateur 'week end' pilot up to operational standards on modern aircraft. As a matter of fact, you never really could; it was only the 'phoney war' period that enabled us to get the Auxiliaries battleworthy by the time of the Battle of Britain.'

Slessor's note was dated 18 May 1951, just after the first nine of the twenty RAuxAF fighter squadrons had been called up for three months of continuous training, in effect creating a pseudo-'phoney war' just in case the Korean business got really out of hand and spread to Europe, which was seen to be a real possibility at the time.[1] Since then the auxiliaries had certainly demonstrated their ability to 'stand to' through their participation in pre-planned exercises. But this rarely involved the whole of each unit and there were recognised limits to this capability. For instance, to quote from HQ Fighter Command's report on the biggest air defence exercise mounted since the war, 1954's Exercise DIVIDEND:

'Inclusion of the Auxiliaries necessitates holding the exercise at week-ends, but Phase II was started on Thursday 22nd July to provide experience in some aspects of the type of situation likely to be met if war started at short notice. In these circumstances it is

[1]It is perhaps worth pointing out that, in 1951, the RAuxAF was in a rather healthier state than its American counterpart. Following their three-month continuous training sessions, all of the British squadrons were fully operational and mounted on jets. It took the Americans twice as long to bring the ANG up to the mark and six Guard squadrons were still flying Mustangs as late as 1957.

unlikely that the Auxiliaries, both flying and ground, would start to come on the scene before some 36 hours had elapsed.'

Reading between the lines of the DIVIDEND report one could also begin to discern the writing on the wall. National defence was becoming increasingly predicated upon the presumption of a no-notice WW III which would soon dictate the maintenance of a rapid response capability on a permanent basis – the Quick Reaction Alert (QRA) concept. It was hardly practical to expect auxiliary units to be able to maintain this level of readiness, of course, and there was little point anyway unless we could afford to provide them with new aeroplanes, which we could not. That being the case, the auxiliary squadrons had to be regarded as an increasingly unaffordable luxury. The fostering scheme had had the potential to permit a few auxiliary pilots to have been involved but, even if it could have been made to work, it is questionable whether it would really have produced what was needed.

Why? Because RAuxAF pilots earmarked to participate in this scheme were allocated only thirty Hunter hours per year, most of which would probably have been accumulated in a concentrated burst during an annual two-week stint of 'continuous training'; the rest of their flying, a notional 100 hours, was to be carried out on Meteors or Vampires. By contrast, a regular fighter pilot of the late 1950s would have expected to clock up about twice as much airborne time annually, and all of it on Hunters. Clearly, even allowing for a period of international tension to permit the RAuxAF to be called out, it would take some time to bring these part-timers up to scratch and such delays were considered to be increasingly unacceptable in the mid-1950s when higher states of readiness were seen to be the coming order of the day. It also has to be said that sustaining the infrastructure to support twenty fighter squadrons was an inordinately expensive way to produce just forty relatively inexperienced Hunter pilots.

Another argument made available to the Secretary of State, but which he also decided not to invoke, concerned manning. Since 1951 the majority of RAF pilots, including National Servicemen (the main source of latter day RAuxAF pilots), had been trained in Canada under a scheme implemented as a response to the Korean War. This arrangement was scheduled to be terminated in 1957 and it was not intended to replace all of this lost capacity with a corresponding expansion of the domestic training organisation. There would, therefore, be a reduction in throughput which would have considerable implications for the manning of the auxiliary squadrons.

So much for what George Ward actually said, or what he could have said. There were, however, other significant developments waiting in the wings of which he must surely have been aware but of which he could not yet speak. Only three months after the announcement of the disbandment of the RAuxAF, Duncan Sandys published his Defence White Paper and a few weeks after that, on 23 May 1957, NATO formally adopted MC14/2, the policy statement which introduced the 'trip wire' strategy. Such fundamental shifts in national and international defence policy would not have been dreamed up overnight or in isolation, of course, and key politicians, senior civil servants and the Chiefs of Staff would all have been well aware of what was being planned.[2] The swingeing cut backs that were in prospect would have put paid to the RAuxAF in any case and it is even possible that it may have been decided to announce its closure in advance so as to minimise the impact of the subsequent announcement which would eventually result in the disbandment of about fifty *regular* squadrons.

So why did the 1957 White Paper make the dissolution of the RAuxAF inevitable? There were three reasons, all of which relate, to some degree, to those which have already been discussed. First, Sandys had concluded that, since there could be no defence against the ballistic missile, which was about to become the primary threat, there was little point in maintaining large numbers of fighters in an attempt to achieve the impossible. This logic, which clearly reflected the philosophy enshrined within NATO's about-to-be-adopted MC14/2, dictated that the only realistic approach would be to create and maintain a nuclear strike force which could demonstrably and convincingly deliver an unacceptably heavy retaliatory response. Such defences as were to be retained, and which were to be largely equipped with guided missiles, would be dedicated to preserving that force, ie the twenty Thor launch sites and the V-bomber main bases.

---

[2] For instance, CAS's personal file on the reappraisal of UK defence policy had been opened as early as June 1956.

Although it had been accepted that Fighter Command could not be expected to protect the UK in war, it was still required to police national airspace and to investigate intruders in peacetime. To do this, however, would require relatively small numbers of interceptors, a handful of which would be held constantly at a high state of readiness. There would simply be no need for twenty additional fighter units manned by part-timers.[3] Had there been a sensible case for keeping the auxiliaries AOCinC Fighter Command, Sir Thomas Pike, would surely have fought to retain them when their withdrawal had first been mooted in mid-1956; but he did not. Indeed, it was HQ Fighter Command's suggestion that it could probably manage without the FCUs as well that effectively sealed the fate of the entire RAuxAF.

Secondly, there was the ever present question of cost. By 1956-57 the UK was having to sustain the extensive rearmament programme which had been triggered by the Korean War whilst simultaneously underwriting the costs of its initial nuclear weapons programme. It had recently been committed to lengthy and expensive (in manpower as well as treasure) campaigns in Korea and Kenya; it was still fighting in Malaya and, through the Suez affair, had just undergone the humiliating experience of being shown its true place in the post-war pecking order. We should also remember that, although there had been some progressive relaxation, wartime rationing had not finally ended until as late as 1954. People had had more than enough of post-war austerity, yet the UK was still spending a disproportionate amount on guns; it was time for some butter, perhaps even a little jam. In 1956-57 the UK was devoting 8% of GNP to defence, down from a post-war peak of 11% in 1953-54, but still far too high compared to France's 6% and the FRG's mere 4%.[4] By this time the continentals had recovered from the devastation of 1945 sufficiently to begin to challenge the UK in the export market but we were hard-pressed to mount a response with 24% of our shipbuilding and

---

[3]In January 1957 Fighter Command could field thirty-five regular squadrons plus the twenty RAuxAF units. Five years later it was down to eleven squadrons of fighters plus eleven Bloodhound Mk 1 sites. By 1965 this had dwindled to seven squadrons and only two Bloodhound Mk 2 sites. Today, there are just four squadrons of Tornado F.3s.

[4]To put this another way, Defence accounted for 30% of public expenditure in the 1956-57 Budget; in the 2002-03 Budget it was less than 6%.

14% of our engineering output already committed to national defence. Defence expenditure simply had to be constrained.

So what implications did this have for the RAuxAF squadrons? Plainly, advances in technology meant that they were bound to become increasingly expensive to equip and maintain. If the defence budget had been unable to run to providing the auxiliaries with Hunters, there could obviously be no question of equipping them with Lightnings – and the Lightning was not that far off, having been flying in prototype form since as early as 1954. That being the case, it was clear that the auxiliaries were simply unaffordable in the long run and the sooner they were closed down the sooner could savings be realised.

There was a cruel paradox here, of course. While the budget had been unable to underwrite Hunters for the auxiliaries in 1956, the White Paper of 1957 would result in a dozen regular Hunter squadrons being disbanded before that year was out; four more went in 1958 and others were to follow. While Hunters had once been a scarce commodity, the air force suddenly found itself with swept-wing fighters to burn, almost literally. But it was too late for the RAuxAF; the ministerial logic that had created this sudden surfeit of Hunters, by concluding that we did not need large numbers of manned fighters, applied equally to the auxiliary squadrons.

Thirdly, there was the manning problem. Another major innovation to be announced by Sandys was the imminent end of conscription. As Tony Freeman explained, the RAuxAF had been heavily dependent upon the National Service system for its personnel, tradesmen as well as pilots, but critically the latter, ever since 1950. The fact is that volunteers, whether straight off the street or ex-regulars, had never joined the auxiliaries in adequate numbers (not even in the fondly remembered halcyon days of the 1930s) and, once the National Service tap had been turned off, the RAuxAF would be living off its fat. With hindsight, it is even arguable that it was actually better to have shut the organisation down while it was still in robust health, rather than having to watch it wither and die.

There were other, more subtle, factors embedded within the manning equation. When the first cohort of auxiliaries had signed on in 1946 and '47 they had been wartime veterans, soldiers, who were, to paraphrase the bard, still prepared to seek 'the bubble reputation, even in the cannon's mouth'. Ten years on, however, these men were entering the fifth of their seven ages. They were becoming magisterial justices 'in fair round belly with good capon lined', or, more to the point, a wife, 2.4 children, a mortgage and the prospect of a partnership. Clearly, it was time to stop pretending to be Biggles and concentrate on the day job. With an increasing proportion of pilots being conscripts, not all of whom signed on for a second stint once they had discharged their three-year reserve obligation, the overall experience level was declining and RAuxAF officers of squadron leader rank became increasingly scarce. In 1947, all twenty COs had been auxiliaries. Four years later it was becoming necessary to use regulars to plug the odd gap. By the end of 1956 twelve of the squadrons were commanded by regulars and that 60% proportion was bound to increase.

It did not end there either. The Air Council had been grappling with a recruiting problem ever since 1945. The ill-conceived 'aircrew' scheme, with its alphanumeric soup of P1s, N2s, S3s and the like had signally failed to attract adequate numbers and had been abandoned in 1950. Thereafter, virtually all pilots (and navigators) were automatically commissioned but (apart from relatively small numbers of Cranwellians and university entrants) on short service terms. This had not proved to be the answer either, because, after the instability of a global depression sandwiched between two world wars, the popular aspiration was for 'a job for life with a pension'. Gradually overcoming its reservations over the age of its pilots, the air force had begun to offer much longer term engagements in 1955 (which also had the advantages of reducing recruiting targets while amortising training costs over much longer periods). By 1960 the '38/16' hitch had become more or less standard, this just as the output of National Servicemen was tailing off. With the supply of young ex-conscripts rapidly drying up, the RAuxAF would have had to recruit its pilots from ex-regulars, most of whom were now going to be pushing 40 years of age. At the time, this would still have been considered far *too* old; it was after all, precisely why the RAF had made 38 the age at which one's services would no longer be required.

In 1956, when the decision to disband the RAuxAF was actually taken, AMP's staff was still (as it always is) grappling with the problems involved in trying to reconcile the conflicting demands of recruiting and retention with those of contemporary terms and conditions of service. The final outcome of these deliberations was still some way off but the way ahead was already discernible; the RAF of the near future would have to become a volunteer force of relatively long-service regulars. It is quite plain, therefore, that, had the auxiliary squadrons not been closed down in 1957 they would have encountered increasing, and probably insurmountable, difficulties in maintaining their strength from 1960 onwards.

Although it does not appear to have been deployed while the disbandment debate was going on, there was actually a fourth argument which fatally weakened the case for retention of the auxiliaries. The principle underlying the existence of the RAuxAF was that it was a force intended for home defence *in extremis* which, in practical terms at least, precluded its use in colonial campaigns, like those in Kenya and Malaya, or in foreign military adventures, like Suez. This constitutional straightjacket meant that there could be no fallback position for the squadrons once they had been rendered redundant by the adoption of the 'trip wire' strategy.

So, to summarise, while a lack of resources (money) may have provided an easily understood, and thus convenient, rationale to justify the disbandment decision to the British public in January 1957, it was actually of secondary importance. The real bottom line was that there would simply be no need for substantial reserve forces under the radically different defence policy that was about to be adopted, but to which overt reference could not yet be made.

The brinkmanship of the 1961 Berlin crisis highlighted the political constraints inherent in the concept of instant mutually assured destruction. A less rigid approach was devised and this was ratified in 1968 with NATO's adoption of the new strategy of 'flexible response', as expressed in MC14/3. But by that time, all other considerations aside, the spiralling cost of defence equipment alone had clearly ruled out any possibility of re-establishing auxiliary flying squadrons in the traditional mould.

While that may have been true for the British, Gp Capt Harris's reference to later American practice does invite some comment. It is, of course, tempting to contrast the RAuxAF with the ANG but I wonder whether that is a valid comparison. While it is true that the Americans are still able to recruit a proportion of Guardsmen off the street and train them to fly from the *ab initio* stage, we know that the RAF has enough problems simply trying to recruit and retain its quota of regulars (it would, I suspect, curl the hair of some of our older members if they knew what blandishments are having to be offered to today's pilots in order to persuade them to stay in uniform). Furthermore, the USAF offers ten-year engagements, which means that many of its pilots have rather more useful mileage left on them when they are discharged than do those of the RAF.

Recruiting factors aside, I believe that the USA is alone in still being able to sustain (afford) autonomous auxiliary flying units. The UK is no superpower, of course, and it would probably be more appropriate to compare its approach to reserve aviators with those of Canada and/or Australia. In broad terms, all three nations have done much the same thing. Having all once maintained flying squadrons within post-war 'citizens air forces' of some description, all three have been obliged to replace such ambitious schemes with more modest arrangements that involve auxiliary aircrew being integrated into regular units as augmentees. This is a relatively low profile solution, of course, but it is both practical and cost-effective.

As a footnote, it might be worth adding that, because George Ward's name crops up fairly frequently, both here and in some of the presentations made on the day, it would be easy to perceive him as being the villain of the piece; but we should, perhaps, avoid shooting the messenger. Before becoming a prominent post-war politician, Ward had spent many years in RAF uniform. Having completed a short service engagement in 1932-37, he was recalled two years later to end the war as a group captain (and an A1 QFI to boot). Perhaps even more significantly, however, he had begun his flying career as an auxiliary, as Plt Off Ward of No 601 Sqn in 1929.

George Ward had been the Parliamentary Under-Secretary of State for Air in 1952-55, but the politicians who actually occupied the key Air Ministry posts while the fate of the RAuxAF was really being settled in 1956 were Nigel Birch and Christopher Soames. A reshuffle meant that Ward returned to the Ministry as Secretary of State (and thus President of the Air Council) on 19 January 1957. Just four days later it was the new Minister's misfortune to have to make the formal disbandment announcement in the House. I imagine that, in view of his Service background, that chore may well have taken some of the initial shine off his recent promotion.

MARITIME HEADQUARTERS UNITS
OF THE ROYAL AUXILIARY AIR FORCE
by Squadron Leader Bruce Blanche

For nearly forty years the three Maritime Headquarters Units (MHUs) of the Royal Auxiliary Air Force provided support to Coastal Command and its successors in a variety of roles. From 1959, these three units constituted the entire RAuxAF until Regiment Squadrons began to be formed some twenty years later. This paper summarises the history of the MHUs, considers the various tasks which they undertook and reviews the ways in which their personnel were trained.

The Maritime Headquarters Units

Following the disbandment of the auxiliary flying squadrons and the various fighter control and ground defence units, the strength of the RAuxAF had been reduced to fewer than 300 personnel. This state of affairs was to last until 1979, during which period a generation of regular RAF personnel had virtually ceased to be aware of the existence of the auxiliaries. The force was kept in being, however, through the foresight of Air Mshl Sir Edward Chilton, then AOCinC Coastal Command, and his Senior Air Staff Officer, AVM Wilf Oulton, who recognised the value of retaining auxiliaries as trained augmentees to supplement the regular staffs at operational HQs. To satisfy this requirement three Maritime Headquarters Units were established to support HQ Coastal Command (subsequently HQs 18 Gp, 11/18 Gp, and currently 3 Gp) at Northwood, and the former Northern and Southern Maritime Air Regions, based at Pitreavie Castle, Fife and at Mount Wise, near Plymouth, respectively.

These three units provided reinforcement and support in the Operations Rooms, Intelligence Sections and Communications Centres of their related HQs, all of which had major NATO, as well as national, responsibilities. A fourth unit, the Ulster Maritime Support Unit, undertook similar duties at Aldergrove between 1960 and 1965 when it was disbanded.

No 1 (County of Hertford) Maritime Headquarters Unit

No 1 MHU was formed in January 1960 under the command of Wg Cdr A R Poole. It was initially manned by officers and airmen of the former No 604 (County of Middlesex) Sqn, No 3604 (County of Middlesex) Fighter Control Unit and No 3700 (County of London) Radar

Reporting Unit. The unit also recruited from Nos 600 (City of London) and 601 (County of London) Sqns and the Reserve Flights of the RAFVR, including No 7301 Flt at Northwood. No 1 MHU's original task was to provide personnel to man the NATO Maritime Headquarters at Northwood (CINCEASTLANT) but it subsequently took on the additional responsibility for supporting the Maritime Headquarters (MHQ) and airfield at Gibraltar as well. For many years the unit was located at Valency House, an Edwardian country house, within sight of Northwood but in 1991 it moved to new purpose-built accommodation at Northolt.

No 1 MHU fostered close links with both the City of London and the Worshipful Company of Butchers. Its badge, with the motto *Swift to Respond*, was approved by HM Queen Elizabeth II in July 1965. The badge was dedicated at St Clement Danes Church in 1970. On 12 June 1989 No 1 MHU was proud to field Fg Off John Easton when the Sovereign's Colour for the Royal Auxiliary Air Force was presented at a parade held at RAF Benson. The RAuxAF was, incidentally, the first reserve formation to be so honoured.

No 2 (City of Edinburgh) Maritime Headquarters Unit

No 2 MHU was formed under the command of Flt Lt R B Worthington on 1 November 1959, its original staff being furnished by officers and airmen drawn from the former No 3603 (City of Edinburgh) Fighter Control Unit, which had disbanded the previous day. The unit's Town Headquarters, formerly that of No 603 Sqn and No 3603 Fighter Control Unit, had been used by the auxiliaries since 1925, and it still is.

The role of the unit on its formation was to provide operations, intelligence and communications personnel to support the joint RN/RAF MHQ at Pitreavie Castle, particularly during NATO exercises. In 1986, the unit's role expanded to include mission support for aircrew operating from Kinloss, Lossiemouth, Machrihanish and Turnhouse. It would eventually take on even more responsibility including the provision of operational, intelligence, medical, regiment, air traffic control and MT personnel to support the operations of the Nimrod force at Kinloss, the maritime attack Tornados at Lossiemouth and the air defence operations of the Tornado F.3 squadrons at Leuchars. In addition, the unit provided intelligence support for the NATO/National Joint Intelligence Centre at the Faslane Naval Base.

To train for these various roles, the unit supported the Joint Maritime Operations Training Staff (JMOTS) during Joint Maritime Courses and also provided support to overseas deployments.

No 2 MHU's Badge, with the motto *Watch Weil*, was approved by HM The Queen in July 1963.

No 3 (County of Devon) Maritime Headquarters Unit

No 3 MHU was formed at Mount Batten in January 1960, its initial members being drawn from No 3512 (County of Devon - Exeter) Fighter Control Unit and No 3513 (County of Devon - Plymouth) Fighter Control Unit under the command of Wg Cdr R E G Van der Kiste. The MHU provided personnel to support HQ 19 Gp at the Joint Maritime Headquarters at Mount Wise. Its commitments were later expanded to embrace Chivenor, Gibraltar and St Mawgan. On the closure of Mount Batten in 1992, the unit moved to St Mawgan whence it continued to support Gibraltar and, to a lesser extent, Mount Wise.

Featuring Drake's drum with the motto *Muster*, No 3 MHU's badge was approved in February 1963

Roles

RAuxAF personnel from the MHUs were established to augment the regular operations, intelligence and communications staffs at HQ Coastal Command during Transition to War (TTW) and during major NATO exercises. Working with their colleagues in the Royal Naval Reserve, the MHU personnel were initially expected to provide the third watch 'down the hole' in the various MHQ bunkers.

MHU personnel also provided expertise in the same fields at Northwood, Gibraltar, Kinloss, Lossiemouth, Machrihanish and St Mawgan. Specific duties included the tasking of maritime patrol, reconnaissance and strike/attack aircraft and the briefing and debriefing of aircrews. The MHUs worked closely together and personnel were often interchanged for their annual training or exercises, particularly in support of the JMOTS at Turnhouse (and later at Northwood), during the three annual Joint Maritime Courses (JMCs) to which the MHUs were committed from 1986 onwards, this activity involving personnel working in a variety of capacities at Pitreavie Castle, Machrihanish and Kinloss.

At much the same time as No 3 MHU moved to St Mawgan in 1992, the locally based Nimrods moved to Kinloss, so the MHU's primary task thereafter became the support of St Mawgan in its new role as a Forward

Operating Base. In addition, it continued to support exercises, with unit personnel augmenting the station's own operations and intelligence staff. The unit also supported the Maritime Cell in the Joint Operations Centre at Gibraltar with taskers, controllers, intelligence officers and clerks, and provided the entire operational support staff at the airfield. In short, Gibraltar was totally dependent upon the officers of No 3 MHU for operations and intelligence support during exercises and they could also be called upon to assist in emergencies, as they did, for instance, in the case of the *Herald of Free Enterprise* disaster.

In addition to their primary specialisations, the MHUs were also expected to furnish some ancillary assistance during TTW, the provision of MT drivers and medical support for instance. Although all MHU personnel had specific war roles, the aim was to train them so that they would be capable of filling both headquarters and station posts, thus giving them the flexibility required for both peacetime exercises and war.

As an example of the latter, MHU personnel provided support at Northwood, Kinloss, St Mawgan, Lossiemouth and Pitreavie Castle during Operation GRANBY, the Gulf War of 1990-91. More recently still, they have supported the RAF effort during operations conducted in Bosnia and Kosovo (Operations ALLIED FORCE, ENGADINE and AGRICOLA).

Personnel and Training

The three MHUs reflected the traditions of the old RAuxAF fighter squadrons, in that each was an independent unit with its own administrative and training structure. The establishment ranged from seventy to one hundred auxiliary personnel, commanded by a wing commander. The rank structure within each MHU was determined by the war appointments of its personnel, eg the CO was expected to fill a Duty Wing Commander Operations slot. Day-to-day running of the unit and training support was handled by a nucleus of regulars headed by an adjutant.

As is customary in the reserve forces, auxiliaries came from many walks of life: teachers; accountants; scientists; engineers; students; public servants; secretaries; train drivers and even members of the Defence Intelligence Staff were but a few of the occupations represented. Some officers and airmen were ex-regulars, among them former aircrew, engineers, nurses, educators, fighter controllers, Regiment gunners and communicators.

The three MHUs followed a similar annual training programme, although training was varied to suit local requirements. A typical training cycle consisted of one training weekend per month, followed by two Sundays and one evening per week (amounting to a minimum attendance of 96 non-continuous hours which is equivalent to twelve days). In order to achieve and maintain the standards set by their regular counterparts, MHU personnel were each allocated fifty-six man-training days, with any individual authorised up to ninety-nine days. All auxiliaries carried out fifteen day's Annual Continuous Training at their war appointments or on courses or detachments.

Additional Voluntary Training could be undertaken if suitable opportunities presented themselves. Finally, all three MHUs participated in an annual 18 Gp-sponsored exercise, Exercise PENNY BLACK, which was designed to test operational procedures and to demonstrate the inter-operability of the MHUs at their TTW locations.

The MHUs adhered to regular RAF training methods and standards. They co-ordinated their efforts to review and restructure their training syllabi, particularly in relation to operations and intelligence, as well as General Service Training, including Common Core Skills (ie first aid, skill at arms, nuclear, biological and chemical procedures and post-attack recovery training). Auxiliary personnel were eligible for rates of pay and expenses similar to those drawn by their regular counterparts and a tax-free Annual Bounty was paid each year on successful completion of training.

Operations and Intelligence Tasks

Most auxiliary MHU officers were commissioned into the General Duties (Ground) Branch (later the Ops Support Branch) in either flight operations or intelligence specialities. At MHQs Operations Officers were primarily concerned with the tasking and control of maritime patrol aircraft. At station level, they briefed and debriefed aircrews.

Similarly, there were two types of intelligence posts. One was at MHQs, during major NATO exercises, for instance, or in support of JMCs. At this level RAuxAF personnel represented a substantial proportion of the intelligence community, working alongside regulars and reservists from other Services, including those of NATO nations. Information on 'enemy' forces reported by ships and aircraft was processed to create the Recognised Maritime Picture (RMP) and used to

*Members of a joint RAuxAF/RNR/TA Ops/Int watch team at Faslane
discuss one of the points arising during JMC 99/2*

produce Air and Flag Staff briefings, periodic maritime intelligence summaries and *ad hoc* intelligence reports.

The station intelligence task involved working closely with maritime aircrew. Operations/Intelligence Officers briefed the crew on the potential threat before their mission and debriefed them on their return. The post-mission report was signalled to the MHQ where it was assessed and integrated into the RMP which was, in turn, relayed to the stations, thus completing a continuous cycle.

Operations/Intelligence Training

MHU Operations and Intelligence personnel frequently attended RN/RAF courses related to maritime operations, alongside their regular counterparts in order to be fully conversant with current levels of risk, operational techniques and tactics. These included courses at the Maritime Tactics School at HMS *Dryad*, Mission Support System courses at RAF Kinloss and intelligence-related courses at the Defence Intelligence and Security School at Ashford and later at RAF Chicksands.

Interlude 1996 - 2000

Although they had been formed to support Coastal Command during the Cold War, the three MHUs continued to provide Strike Command's HQ 18 Gp with a similar service in the dangerous and uncertain situation that took the place of the relative stability of the east-west confrontation which had ended with the collapse of the USSR in 1991. The optimism sparked by the demise of the Warsaw Pact meant that it was almost inevitable that there would be cut backs in defence spending and 'Options for Change' and the subsequent Strategic Defence Review led to some early reductions in RAuxAF manpower followed, in 1996, by the announcement that Pitreavie Castle, Turnhouse, Mount Wise and Mount Batten were all to be closed.

While No 1 MHU continued to support the NATO HQ at Northwood, the closure of the MHQs at Pitreavie Castle and Mount Wise had deprived Nos 2 and 3 MHUs of their main functions. Largely operating on their own initiative, the personnel of the two notionally redundant units exploited other avenues and found continuing employment in support of the periodic JMCs, sundry maritime exercises and the air defence operations of the two fighter squadrons at Leuchars.

The upshot of this was that the MHUs gradually evolved into what amounted to 'Maritime Support Squadrons', each still having much the same establishment as before. While continuing to provide operational support staff for maritime HQs and squadrons, their commitments broadened to embrace mission support for the Sentry and for Air-to-Air Refuelling (AAR).

Among other innovations, the new Reserve Forces Act of 1996 had made provision for reservists to work full-time and to be employed on peace-keeping and humanitarian operations. It was this new flexibility that permitted MHU personnel to be deployed to Italy and Germany in support of Operation ALLIED FORCE, to Kosovo for Operation AGRICOLA and to Saudi Arabia for Operation JURAL.

Re-roling and Re-formation

During 1999, the Air Force Board granted a request, made by Lord Monro in his capacity as Honorary Inspector General, that new squadrons of the expanding RAuxAF should be allocated the identities of some of the auxiliary squadrons that had been disbanded in 1957, thus reinstating their number plates and badges.

On 1 October 1999, the Queen approved the re-formation of No 603 (City of Edinburgh) Sqn from the personnel of No 2 MHU and of No 600 (City of London) Sqn from the personnel of Nos 1 and 3 MHUs.

No 600 Sqn's role was to provide trained augmentation personnel for any HQ handling RAF or joint operations anywhere, but specifically including the national Permanent Joint Headquarters and within CINCEASTLANT's NATO HQ, both of which are at Northwood, and on the staff of the Joint Force Air Component Commander at High Wycombe. The squadron could offer specialists in the fields of intelligence, flight operations, communications, logistics support, motor transport and administration.

The new No 603 Sqn has a specialist Survive to Operate role. Alongside logistics and air operations, the squadron's primary role is now a vital element in the operational capacity of the RAF. Survive to Operate and Force Protection are now integral elements of current NATO(Air) and RAF doctrine, which embrace the defence and protection of assets involved in expeditionary operations. In addition, the squadron continues to provide mission support for maritime and other RAF and NATO(Air) formations or units, wherever and whenever this may be required in peace or war.

Contribution

For twenty years the personnel of the MHUs were the sole representatives of the RAuxAF and, as such, they provided the foundations upon which the present force was built, starting in 1979 with the formation of some auxiliary Regiment squadrons in the wake of the Soviet invasion of Afghanistan. Indeed, it is arguable that, without the example of the MHUs on which to build, there might not be a Royal Auxiliary Air Force today.

FORTY YEARS IN VOLUNTEER SERVICE
by **Group Captain Peter Harris.**

My aim is to give a personal view of what it was like to be a Volunteer
Reservist and an Auxiliary over a time span of almost forty years, from
the start of the 1950s through to the late 1980s, and hopefully to convey
an impression of the enthusiasm for part-time service which we
possessed then, and which I am sure our successors still do today. I also
hope to be able to demonstrate the evolution of the Auxiliary ethos which
took place during my service, as well as briefly covering some of the
more difficult administrative problems faced by those at the top.

Flying With The RAFVR

On going up to Birmingham University in 1949, after completing
nearly two years statutory service in the Royal Air Force, I soon learnt
that the best club there was the UAS; I immediately applied to join, and
was indoctrinated still further in military aviation by my CO, Sqn Ldr
Aiken, now of course Air Chf Mshl Sir John. Most of us had already
completed National Service, RAF University Scholarships had not yet
come into being, and we were all in the RAFVR. Attendance for flying
training during term-time meant a journey across Birmingham, from
Edgbaston in the south-west to Castle Bromwich in the north-east, for
which we had to use our own transport, in my case a bicycle, but
nevertheless it was a great diversion from the lecture room, laboratory or
private study time, both during the week and at the weekend. During the
long summer vacation, and sometimes at Easter, we deployed for two
weeks to an RAF station where our ground lectures and flying training
could be more concentrated.

After graduation, now commissioned into the RAFVR, I continued
flying, first at the Panshanger Reserve Flying School near Hatfield, and
subsequently at Hornchurch and Redhill. Together with my older post-
WW II colleagues I held the view that the Reserve Flying Schools of the
1950s were extremely convivial and enjoyable flying clubs which we
were privileged to be paid to belong to. We turned up at weekends
whenever we wished, as well as for our annual fortnight's 'summer
camp', spending a good many hours passing our time away in the crew
room waiting for a flight, the pilots in Tiger Moths, Chipmunks or
whatever, the navigators in Ansons, and hopefully not being clamped in

First solo, at Woodvale with Birmingham UAS April 1948.

by bad weather. The lengthy journeys most of us had to make to reach our designated airfield were of no consequence to us if we were to get in some flying.

With the benefit of both hindsight and maturity, it is easy to understand why our flying activities were progressively curtailed in the mid-1950s and eventually cancelled. From a military standpoint, the RAFVR did represent a pool from which individuals could be called up if the need arose, as occurred during the Korean War, but the post-war auxiliary fighter squadrons were of more immediate use, being equipped with jets and trained to provide a highly-skilled reserve for Fighter Command, and even they were to fall under the axe only two years later. Although we shared their dismay and disappointment when our weekend activities were brought to an abrupt close, I believe we all retained our enthusiasm and dedication to the concept of reserve service, and were ready when the phoenix eventually arose from the ashes, albeit in a different form.

Although I transferred immediately to what was then the Technical (Signals) Branch, with a war appointment at HQ 2nd TAF at München Gladbach in Germany, my training commitment was to attend for only two weeks a year; I must admit that this limited involvement did not generate the same level of enthusiasm, and not long after my first attendance I was put on the non-training list, as for the next few years my civilian job was going to take me to some remote parts of the world, including Christmas Island, the UK H-bomb trials site in the central Pacific, where I made some long-lasting Service friends with whom I was to come into contact later in life, amongst them Barry Newton, now an air vice-marshal and Honorary Inspector-General of the Royal Auxiliary Air Force.

Lean Auxiliary Times

While I was a UAS cadet I had been attracted to the auxiliaries, and when it was decided to establish the Maritime Headquarters Units (MHUs), the opportunity arose to join them, albeit not in the flying role which I had enjoyed earlier. Early in 1960 I transferred from the RAFVR to the RAuxAF, joining No 1 MHU at Northwood as a flying officer Signals Officer and virtually a founder-member. I later transferred to Intelligence, remaining with the unit until 1978, the last six years as its CO in the rank of wing commander.

It was originally envisaged that, in the event of war, MHU personnel would form the third watch 'down the hole', although, because we had our own accountant, equipment, medical and Regiment officers, as well as clerks, cooks, drivers, medical orderlies, stewards and storekeepers, we actually had the potential to operate as a self-contained unit. In practice, however, skill levels were very variable in the early days, as was the experience of many of the regulars who were drafted in as war reinforcements. As a result, we soon found ourselves distributed between all three watches. This meant that we worked more closely with our regular counterparts and we had to train hard to match their standards. I thought then, and I still do, that, having trained for these tasks throughout the year, many of us actually achieved a standard of local knowledge and proficiency which surpassed that of some of the regulars who descended into the 'hole' for only a few days each year.

The training strategy was that the officers would train the senior NCOs, who in turn would train the juniors; the regular training staff in each unit provided the necessary course material and maintained the records, whilst the staff in the NATO sections that we were supporting assisted with specialist training wherever and whenever it was required. Any tendency towards the relaxed 'crew room' atmosphere associated with the old flying squadrons was soon dispelled by the allocation of a wide range of secondary duties, which kept us fully occupied throughout every evening and weekend training period.

Each CO was responsible for recruiting and for bringing his unit up to the standard of operational efficiency required to discharge its responsibilities; to this end he could set his own attendance demands. Training schedules were developed independently, to meet local civilian employment and transport factors, but the overall attendance time considerably exceeded the minimum required by the regulations. This arrangement worked well, even if, in some instances, like my own with respect to both signals and intelligence, personnel had little or no previous experience of their task and a considerable amount of self-training 'on the job' became essential. Our skills were put to the test during the annual NATO autumn exercise, be it live or 'paper'. In the early years these exercises tended to be of only a few days duration so the MHUs would deploy to one of Coastal Command's airfields for the remainder of their 'summer camp'. This permitted us to complete our General Service Training and also provided us with an opportunity to at least see an aeroplane!

On becoming a Flight Commander, I soon realised the importance of keeping the team fully occupied; this was no problem during recruit and basic training, and when airmen were being trained for promotion, but exchange visits and adventure/expedition training were essential later as morale-boosters. In order to maximise the use of available manpower and to increase our flexibility, we sometimes deployed to one of the other Maritime Headquarters, both during the formal annual exercises and for less high profile exercises at other times of the year. Having become skilled in our particular specialisation, it was not unusual to spend additional time in an appropriate post elsewhere; I have very happy memories of filling the Station Intelligence Officer slot at North Front whilst the regular incumbent took two weeks' home leave at the time of the 1966 World Cup football final!

Having a NATO role, we were effectively isolated from the 'national' teams at our respective headquarters; in my personal experience, this was particularly true of the Intelligence Officers in the Northwood unit. As a consequence, we did not have an opportunity to participate in live operational activity; although our NATO sponsors did brief us on the events and progress of the Cuban missile crisis, and later on the progress of the Soviet Northern Fleet's annual summer exercises. We were not called up, however, and our offer to attend for extra 'training' at weekends, which we would have been glad to undertake, was not taken up either. The logic of this was doubtless that the regular staff would have had to spend time bringing us up to speed, when their energies were concentrated on keeping tabs on the Soviets – and even in the maritime world a lot can happen in a few days.

No 1 MHU had its own premises at Valency House, close to, but outside, the perimeter of the Northwood HQ; No 2 MHU had a similar off base facility. Rather than being part of the MOD estate, these properties actually belonged to the appropriate county or regional Territorial and Auxiliary Forces Association (later to become the Territorial, Auxiliary and Volunteer Reserve Association and, ultimately, the present-day Reserve Forces and Cadet Association). As a result, we had security of tenure. Having discrete accommodation provided us with independent administrative and training accommodation and, and just as importantly, autonomous messes. Separate messes are vital social amenities in an auxiliary organisation, because they permit personnel to relax and socialise with their own comrades once training is over, a well-proven concept within the earlier generation of RAuxAF units and throughout the Territorial Army. Having our own mess meant that the officers were able to hold regular guest nights, the necessary domestic support being provided by the unit's own staff, with, for example, operations clerks and teleprinter operators voluntarily doubling up as stewards. We considered ourselves very fortunate in this regard, especially when compared to our colleagues at Mount Batten who lacked individual mess facilities. To compensate for this No 3 MHU pioneered the idea of the all-ranks club which would, in the fullness of time, became the norm for later auxiliary units.

Because it was juxtaposed with the Command Headquarters, and relatively close to both the Ministry of Defence and High Wycombe, No 1 MHU took on a PR role for the RAuxAF as a whole, frequently entertaining high-ranking officers from both locations. Because our mess was 'outside the fence', we were, of course, able to do much of this without becoming too heavily embroiled in the usual protocol. The RAuxAF was under close scrutiny throughout this period, because, beyond the confines of HQ Coastal Command/18 Group, there were no longer many desk-level staff officers with any direct knowledge and experience of the auxiliaries; indeed there were very few serving *air* officers with such background knowledge. This high-level PR activity, undertaken enthusiastically by unit members at all levels, demonstrated the dedication and sense of elitism which had been inherited from the fighter squadrons, and I would venture to claim that it helped materially to ensure the continued existence of the RAuxAF.

From a personal viewpoint, it was not only the professional task and the honour of eventually being in command that were satisfying and enjoyable during those MHU years. Colleagues took display and recruiting stands to various shows within our area, but I was privileged to participate in a variety of prestigious ceremonial duties: as a flight lieutenant, regularly leading the RAuxAF detachment at the Remembrance Day parade at the Cenotaph in Whitehall and, as a squadron leader, one of the four Reserve Forces officers who had the honour of leading the Lord Mayor's Procession in London during the early 1970s. The greatest privilege of all occurred in 1977, when, as a wing commander, I commanded the 'light blue' contingent at the Royal Silver Jubilee Reserve and Cadet Forces' Review at Wembley Stadium. Being the junior service, we were first to emerge from the players' tunnel and the huge roar of applause was as though we were the England soccer team; as the 'captain', I immediately felt three inches taller, and I got my name on the dust jacket of the subsequent recording of the event as well!

Expansion and Inspectorial Years

The spadework done over a period of several years by my predecessor as Inspector, Gp Capt 'Robbie' Robins, and his Honorary Inspector-General Sir Peter Vanneck, eventually bore fruit with the formation of three Regiment Field Squadrons in 1979, and I was privileged to preside over the next stage as Inspector from 1983 onwards, initially with Sir Peter and then under the highly-valued guidance and tutelage of Air Chf Mshl Sir John Barraclough. Still a part-timer myself, and with 'advice to the Air Force Board, and liaison with Command and Group Headquarters, on RAuxAF matters' as my Terms of Reference, it was both fascinating and satisfying to be part of the expansion process, and to see what could be achieved by 'weekenders'. Over the next few years, a wide range of new roles and activities was to open up, necessitating a more professional approach than ever if the Force was to provide the intended level of support to the RAF. I am sure that my successors will have had very similar experiences during their tours of duty.

The MHUs had already adapted to the introduction of computers, and the evolving roles of the headquarters which they supported; new skills had been learned, remustering to new trades had been successfully achieved, and the process was to continue as the units took on new roles elsewhere within 18 Group.

The reborn No 2503 (County of Lincoln) Sqn immediately revived the old RAuxAF traditions, probably because it had an 'old' number plate, and partly perhaps because of the strong Territorial and Auxiliary ethos which its officers brought with them. In particular, although there were only five officers in the squadron, they sustained the traditional social connection with the county community. These squadrons also maintained the traditional concept of operating as 'formed units', becoming vital components of their stations' defence assets.

The Falklands War demonstrated the need for a trained reserve of movements teams, and led to the formation of No 4624 (County of Oxford) Sqn at Brize Norton. This was conceived to operate on a basis similar to that developed in the MHUs, its 200 personnel being grouped together in small flights, which could deploy either fully or partially when the need arose, trained members frequently being detached for actual operations, not only to Lyneham, but also to RAF bases throughout the world, a concept which proved itself both operationally and in terms of the enthusiasm which it generated amongst the squadron personnel. No 4624 Sqn was also extremely fortunate in being able to nominate a former No 601 Sqn pilot, by then a captain of industry and one of the local gentry, to become its first Honorary Air Commodore; he demonstrated, once again, the great importance of selecting the right individual to fill such a post, in that, through his dedication and support, of not only the CO but the whole squadron, he did a great deal to foster a strong team spirit in the best traditions of the Force, as well as being able to represent his squadron in the community.

The second outcome of the Falklands War was the Aeromedical Evacuation Squadron, which, in my view, did not really achieve its full potential until it moved to Hullavington, where it had appropriate self-contained accommodation. Like its movements neighbours, this squadron operated as individuals and small teams, building on what had gone before, and demonstrated very clearly the flexibility which I am sure still exists in the Force today.

Like the auxiliary Regiment field squadrons, the unique SHORAD squadron formed to defend Waddington, using guns, radars and ammunition captured from the Argentinians, operated as a cohesive formed unit, playing a vital role on its parent base and becoming something of a showpiece for the Force.

The last units to be formed during my tenure of office were the Defence Flights at High Wycombe and Lyneham (STC), and Brampton and St. Athan (RAFSC). These were intended to be a low-cost guard force for their parent stations, with a restricted training commitment compared with the rest of the Force. It was a valuable experiment, but it soon became clear that the auxiliary personnel actually wanted a commitment to more, rather than less, training time, demonstrating that part-timers do have a very special ethos and motivation of their own.

The various roles and the different training and operating regimes introduced during this period demonstrated the flexibility available with auxiliary units and squadrons, and their ability to adapt to changing needs. The introduction of inter-unit competition, in particular through the Robins and Strickland Trophies, did much to promote enthusiasm and performance, building on the traditions of such sought-after prizes as the Esher Trophy competed for by auxiliary fighter squadrons before WW II.

But there was another side to it, and disappointment, if not frustration, was often paramount as new concepts for the use of auxiliaries were slow to get established or never materialised: a return to flying duties, manning of Rapier squadrons by auxiliaries, and the raising of squadrons to fulfil EOD roles come to mind as examples. The experience of the USAF Reserve and of the Royal Hong Kong Auxiliary Air Force, both of which trained *ab initio* pilots for primary operational duties, were brushed aside without any obvious proper consideration. Moreover, bureaucracy and legal, if not political correctness reared their ugly heads. AP 968, 'Regulations for the Royal Auxiliary Air Force', was rewritten in the 1980s to exclude some of its archaic pre-WW II provisions, but in doing so it became only too clear that the Reserve Forces Act prevented RAuxAF personnel, unlike their RAFVR colleagues, from being ordered to undertake certain activities, including going overseas for 'summer camp', a highly-valued reward and in some instances a necessity if suitable training facilities were going to be utilised. We were ingenious enough to get round this by ensuring that all concerned volunteered! Neither was it legal for RAuxAF personnel to be deployed in support of warlike operations, either in the UK or overseas, without a Queen's Order in Council, which politicians wished to avoid. I earlier touched on the unwillingness of NATO and the RAF to use auxiliaries during the Cuban crisis and the Soviet Navy summer exercises; although I was not directly involved at the time, I believe the enthusiastic help offered by auxiliaries during the Falklands War had to be provided at a low key, without any publicity, because of an apparent official reluctance by the RAF to accept such assistance. After much lobbying, largely by the Territorial, Auxiliary and Volunteer Reserve Associations (TAVRA), factors such as these eventually led to the introduction of a new Reserve Forces Act, which did allow auxiliaries to play a useful part in the Gulf War, Yugoslavia and elsewhere.

The ending of the Cold War and the economic difficulties facing business and industry in the 1980s had a marked effect on the willingness of employers to allow their staff time off for military training, especially if it was not clear that they were making a positive contribution to our defence. Small firms could not afford the loss of manpower for two weeks every year, and the banks and large industrial companies which had historically been very supportive, became less generous – and as a business executive as well as Inspector, I experienced both sides of the argument! The TAVRAs and the specially-formed National Employers' Liaison Committee took on the vital task of encouraging employer support; certificates were presented by Lords Lieutenant in appropriate cases, executives were invited to view and to participate in teamwork training, and much stress was placed on the benefits of leadership, teamwork, new technical skills and even first aid training which reservist employees brought back to their civilian workplace.

Resolution of these problems without any staff to do the spadework necessitated the allocation of considerable time; in the light of the subsequent growth in the RAuxAF Inspectorate staff, it is difficult to believe that we coped – or did we leave a lot undone?

The Motivation

Finally, it is perhaps worth looking at what makes auxiliaries tick, because, at the end of the day, if their aspirations are not met, recruits will be hard to come by, and those who do join will not stay and valuable training time will have been wasted – and we must remember that they have a civilian job to do, as well as family commitments to uphold.

In my case, it was initially the opportunity to learn to fly, and then the camaraderie, the challenge of command – by which time the RAuxAF was very much in my blood – and the privilege of being part of an expansion process. I well remember being asked by one senior regular officer why I and so many others gave up our weekends in this way; my response was to compare it with his golfing activity – we were both changing from our weekday working life to an enjoyable and satisfying weekend hobby. At that time, pay was not an important factor of itself, and indeed most of us ploughed back any earnings over the bår after training; it is now many years since I doffed my uniform, and I am not fully up-to-date, but I would hope that extra cash is still not the primary motivation.

I remain convinced that the most important factor for newcomers is the opportunity to do something interesting and worthwhile in their spare time: essential operational tasks, reinforcement during peacetime exercises and actual warlike operations are probably of greater significance than the particular role. The specific words 'serving the nation' are not high on the list of declared aims, perhaps because they sound too pious, although when the need arises, auxiliaries are of course keen to be involved as fully as possible; whether the Gulf War and Yugoslavia have altered this is for someone else to say, but I hope that those who were involved in those conflicts have viewed their time as being a valuable experience. Geographical separation from home or place of work is not necessarily a problem, and I was always impressed by how many officers and airmen travelled considerably further than the 50-mile limit for which travelling allowance was paid.

Maybe it all boils down to the one word 'service', with a small 's'.

THE ROYAL HONG KONG AUXILIARY AIR FORCE
by Air Vice-Marshal Geoffrey Cairns

Among the many aspects of reserve and auxiliary service that we failed to address during the seminar, was the contribution made by the colonies, notably in the Far East where the Straits Settlements (later Malayan) Volunteer Air Force was established as early as 1936, a similar organisation being set up in Burma in 1940. Both operated, chiefly in the light communications role, until their remnants were absorbed into the RAF in 1942. An Air Component had also been added to The Hong Kong Volunteer Defence Force in 1939 but, inevitably, this succumbed to the Japanese in December 1941. After the war Auxiliary Air Forces were set up in Malaya and Hong Kong, the former eventually providing the basis for the Royal Malayan Air Force when it formed in 1958, while the latter continued to function until almost the end of the colonial era when it was reconstituted into a more appropriate form prior to its transfer to the incoming Chinese administration. The following paper must serve as recognition of all of this overseas activity. Ed

When, in 1947, the post-war British Military Government completed its period of administration and the Hong Kong Government resumed its rule, it was clear that the colony was still in need of a local force to assist in its defence. Consequently the Hong Kong Defence Force Ordinance came into effect on 1 May 1949, under which three separate branches were formed: The Hong Kong Regiment (The Volunteers); The Hong Kong Royal Naval Reserve and The Hong Kong Auxiliary Air Force (HKAAF). The Hong Kong Women's Auxiliary Air Force was created at the same time.

In 1949 concern was mounting over the Communist takeover in China, and trouble was soon to move south to the Hong Kong border. It was then decided that the HKAAF was to become a fighter support unit. In furtherance of this policy Flt Lt Derek Rake arrived in Hong Kong from the UK in October 1949. He had been briefed personally by the CinC FEAF and was instructed to report directly to the AOC Hong Kong. His task was to establish an auxiliary squadron modelled on those of the RAuxAF in the UK. It was to have its own servicing support, a Headquarters unit and a Fighter Control Unit, and be a self-sufficient organisation capable of working alongside the RAF.

The last of the HKAAF's Spitfire F.24s, seen here displayed at Kai Tak in 1980, has been with the IWM collection at Duxford since 1989.

Eager ex-servicemen of all nationalities enrolled in the HKAAF and 'wings' of the RAF, RNZAF, RAAF, RCAF, Indian, Dutch, South African and Chinese Air Forces were all to be found on their new uniforms.

Qualified pilots flew Spitfire 18s of No 28 Sqn and subsequently the Mk 24s of No 80 Sqn when the latter was re-equipped with Hornets. However, to sustain the flying unit in the longer term it was necessary to train locally enlisted personnel *ab initio*, and to this end four Austers and four Harvards were acquired. Two RAF QFIs were seconded for the flying instruction task, one of them acting as unit adjutant. In due course some twenty pilots were available to fly the Spitfires, up to six of which were kept serviceable. The unit was affiliated to No 601 Sqn RAuxAF in 1954. Standards were checked annually by the Central Flying School's examiners.

By 1955 the situation on the border had become more stable and it was decided to abandon the plan to re-equip the HKAAF with ex-No 28 Sqn Vampires. Consequently the Spitfires, along with No 80 Sqn's Hornets, were withdrawn after the Queen's Birthday Flypast in April of that year.

The threat to close down the HKAAF entirely was lifted, however, when serious disturbances occurred in Kowloon and the Austers and Harvards proved to be of considerable use in providing aid to the civil powers and, particularly, in support of the HK Police. These activities quickly expanded to search and rescue by land and sea, fire fighting control, anti-smuggling, illegal immigration control and assistance in many forms to outlying and remote areas. It was thus that the HKAAF quickly made itself indispensable. Nevertheless, it had always been appreciated that the rugged terrain of Hong Kong, its New Territories and outlying islands imposed serious limitations on the capabilities of fixed wing aircraft in these new roles, and at the instigation of Gordon Bell of the Royal Observatory of Hong Kong (and soon to become the unit's CO and eventually its Honorary Air Commodore), the HK Government was persuaded to purchase two Widgeon helicopters. These became operational in February 1958 and were replaced by Alouettes in August 1965.

Over the years the Harvards and the Austers were gradually replaced in the training role, first by two Beechcraft Musketeers then by Bulldogs and, eventually, by the Slingsby Firefly. A Britten-Norman Islander was acquired in 1972 to extend the range of off-shore search and rescue tasks and to undertake aerial survey work. This aircraft was equipped with radar capable of locating small ships at a range of forty miles, a variety of SAR communication and navigation equipment, and a wide-angle Swiss RL10 survey camera. This latter, and expensive, facility was widely used for land surveillance during the colony's rapid development. By 1979, with the Vietnamese refugee problem getting out of hand, a Cessna 404 Titan Courier was obtained to support the Islander.

The Royal Hong Kong Defence Force had been disbanded in 1970, the Hong Kong Regiment and the HKAAF thenceforth becoming 'Royal' institutions in their own right. The RHKAAF was awarded a Squadron Standard by Her Majesty The Queen in June 1973. This award was made ahead of the usual twenty-five years as a result of the squadron 'having earned the Sovereign's appreciation for especially outstanding operations'.

As time went by, and with the Hong Kong economy booming, millions of dollars were allocated to the RHKAAF which rapidly increased in effectiveness. The Alouettes were replaced by much more capable Aerospatiale Dauphins in 1980. The Titan and Islander were replaced by a pair of Beech Super King Air B200Cs in 1987-88. These aircraft were part of a massive expansion and reorganisation programme in anticipation of the demilitarisation of the RHKAAF and its incorporation as a Civilian Department of the HK Government, a necessary preparation for the handover of Hong Kong to The People's Republic of China which wished to retain the flying service after June 1997.

Eight Sikorsky S-76s were purchased in 1990 as the Dauphins were retired. The final addition to the fleet being a pair of Sikorsky S-70A Black Hawks.

The RHKAAF was officially disbanded in March 1993 when it became the Government Flying Service (GFS). During its final phase the number of volunteers was run down as it became necessary to employ more and more full time personnel in order to run a 24-hour service. The full strength of the RHKAAF at the closing ceremony was sixteen aircraft and 250 personnel. Only forty-five of the latter were active volunteers but they were all to be absorbed into an auxiliary section of the future GFS where they would be led by the last CO of the RHKAAF, Wg Cdr Dicky Yip. So the tradition lingers on.

At the formal disbandment parade the salute was taken by the Governor, Chris Patten. The event was witnessed by former auxiliary personnel from all over the world, a dinner that evening being attended by more than 400 people. On 31 March 1993 the Standard was laid up in St John's Cathedral by a previous CO, High Court Judge and Hon Air Commodore, Ross Penlington.

The RHKAAF had always been a buoyant unit full of memorable characters reflecting the varied nature of Hong Kong itself. In such a short article it is impossible to recall the many instances of bravery and derring-do. The typhoon season alone accounted for many notable operations. Eight lives are recorded on the unit's Roll of Honour.

It would be invidious to attempt to single out individual contributions from the many which helped to nurture this little acorn permitting it to mature and grow to become a substantial oak tree. Nevertheless, I will mention just two: Danny Cheung, a local youth who was recruited as a cadet in 1954, eventually to become Sqn Ldr Danny Cheung MBE AFC AE; and Sqn Ldr John Shawcross MBE, a full-time government officer and the RHKAAF's Chief Staff Officer, who was responsible for steering the squadron through many of its expansion and re-equipment programmes.

Acknowledgement: *Winged Dragon* (Odyssey, 1996) by Valerie Penlington whose husband Ross was, incidentally, the last Honorary Air Commodore of the RHKAAF.

RECOLLECTIONS OF CAMBRIDGE UAS
AND GLIDING IN THE ATC
by Gp Capt Hans Neubroch

Harvard KF735 of CUAS.

During 1954/55 I was Chief Flying Instructor at Cambridge University Air Squadron. We were established for eleven Chipmunks and four Harvards to provide training for 100 pilots and, uniquely, two Ansons to cater for twenty navigators. In addition, there was a reserve commitment for members who had qualified as fighter controllers during their national service and, for training up to PFB standard, we had a number of technical cadets who, having completed their first year at Henlow, were reading for their engineering degrees. That they achieved their flying qualification was amply shown when they put up a four-Chipmunk formation over the West Country hamlet where one of their number was being married. During my time about half of the pilot members qualified for their PFBs. The Harvard enabled us to train some of these up to full wings standard, and to my knowledge six members qualified, after passing their final handling tests and ground exams at No 3 FTS at Feltwell. One of these went on to CFS and completed a two-year tour as a QFI with the squadron – all without having any form of reserve liability. The navigators followed a special syllabus which included weekend cross-countries to the Channel Islands. None qualified for the navigator's PFB, indeed I was not even aware that there was such a qualification or badge.

In the context of regular recruiting, we measured output in terms of quality rather than quantity in those days. In 1955, one in ten of all air

Chipmunk WK642 of CUAS.

officers then serving had joined the RAF via CUAS. During my time with the squadron we were recruiting only two or three members per year into the air force, although one of these (the then Officer Cadet A Skingsley) eventually rose to four-star rank.

And now a footnote to the story of the RAFVR. During the seminar, passing reference was made to the fact that the VR provided officers for the Air Training Corps and RAF Sections of the Combined Cadet Force, but no mention was made of ATC gliding schools. In the early 1950s there were then some forty-nine such schools throughout the UK, under the control of Reserve and then Home Command, operating mostly at weekends and staffed by instructors commissioned in the Training Branch of the RAFVR, or appointed as civilian instructors.

Up till then most gliding training had been carried out by the solo method, which enabled pupils to handle a basic single-seater. Launches were provided either by a truck or a modified balloon winch, from which a cable was connected to the glider. Cadets progressed through a series of slides and low hops to high hops, from which it might be possible to achieve the 30 seconds' glide required for an 'A' Certificate. These flights were all straight ahead, no turns being involved; but the 'B' Certificate required a flight lasting at least one minute and incorporating an S-turn. In practice this involved a full launch to at least 700 ft, from which it was possible to complete a circuit. Only the more promising cadets were taken to that stage.

This method of instruction had been in use since well before the war and many of the instructors were expert at coaxing cadets into the air, and through their certification, without themselves ever getting airborne, save

Fuzzy, but interesting; one of CUAS's two Anson T.21s VV884.

perhaps for the odd air test. Their knowledge of the theory of flight was often quite rudimentary: one enduring myth claimed that gliders should be turned without banking! Accordingly, there were some spectacular accidents, some of which claimed the lives of cadets – and so a better way was sought.

By the early 1950s two-seater gliders were coming into use, enabling cadets to be given dual before they went solo. But that, in turn, required instructors to be capable, not only of flying themselves, but also of giving the correct sequence of instruction. To bring this transformation about, a gliding instructors' school was established at RAF Detling with training based on a manual of instruction along CFS lines.

Other developments raised standards throughout the organisation, including a soaring camp for advanced cadets during the summer in Derbyshire, where a number completed five-hour flights, and ATC gliding instructors taking part in the National Gliding Championships. Also, elementary gliders were issued to selected RAF Sections of the Combined Cadet Corps.

Others might be able to expand on the subsequent development of ATC gliding, which gave thousands of youngsters their first experience of what it meant to be in control of an aircraft, however primitive. One such 'primitive' may be seen suspended from the ceiling as you climb the stairs to the RAF Museum's auditorium.

RESERVE SCHOOL RECOLLECTIONS

by C Nepean Bishop

This article was first published in Flight *for 19 March 1954 and it is reproduced here by kind permission of the current Editor of* Flight International. *The author was clearly moved to put pen to paper by the imminent closure of No 15 RFS, a casualty of the rapid run down of the post-war RAFVR. In so doing, he hoped that the work of this unit, and the others of, what he refers to as, the 'civilian air force' would 'find its own niche in the annals of Royal Air Force history'. I am not sure that it really has done but, since the article is directly related to the training of reserve aircrew, its reproduction here as a supplementary paper serves both to amplify the proceedings of the Society's recent seminar while going some way towards reminding us how things were actually done a half-century or more since.* **Ed**

The history of 'No 15', one of the latest and last Reserve Flying Schools to be massacred by the present Government, dates back to 1936 when it was announced in the enlightened Parliament of that time that a number of Royal Air Force Reserve Centres were to be brought into operation; one of these was to be at Redhill, where the flying was, as now, controlled by British Air Transport Ltd, with Fg Off (as he was then) A G Douglas, RAFO, as managing director.

Matters were duly organised and after various political and policy vicissitudes, No 15 Elementary and Reserve Flying Training School opened on 3 July 1937, at the same time as No 14 at Castle Bromwich and No 16 at Shoreham. 'No 15' was one of the first group of purely Volunteer Reserve units, as opposed to the existing elementary schools, which had normally catered for short-service-commissioned entrants and had taken on Volunteer Reserve training some three months earlier.

For the whole of its career the school has been operated by the personnel of British Air Transport Ltd, owners of Redhill airfield, and at the time of inauguration was under the management of Fg Off Douglas.

The first chief instructor was Flt Lt I G E ('Dorothy') Dale, RAFO, who had as his regular assistant Fg Off R D ('Bill') Adams, also of the Reserve of Air Force Officers. In addition, there were two extra instructors who functioned at week-ends, when the school was at its busiest.

The first aircraft to be allocated to No 15 were somewhat peculiarly described on paper as 'Gipsy 1 Tiger Moths' and these were collected during the week-end that the school opened, turning out to be a number of somewhat weary metal-fuselage DH Gipsy Moths! These the chief AID Inspector of the time promptly put unserviceable, he having no maintenance schedules for the type; and the CFI, a man not of light build, declared that if he was to fly these contraptions he would need to be issued with a pair of wire-cutters, without which speedy exodus from the front seat, in case of emergency, would be well-nigh impossible. He also pointed out that the performance of these aircraft with full fuel tanks and two heavy passengers would leave much to be desired.

All these objections were, however, overruled by the Air Ministry and Reserve Command (as Flying Training Command was then known[1]), and flying started to schedule. In point of fact, the DH 60s were only replaced by Magisters some fifteen months later, and after they had flown a total of some 3997 hours. The first two Hawker Harts arrived in October 1937 and just over 1500 hours were flown on the two types before the end of the year. Fifty-two Volunteer Reservists were attached to the school at that time.

1938 saw the pupil strength of the school increased to 115 VRs who had fourteen Magisters and fourteen Hart variants in which to fly, the former having by now taken the place of the even more weary Moths. A total of 6300 hours was completed during the year, the peak month being July, when the elementary types flew 340 hours and the Harts 525. By December the instructor strength was up to nine, and during that month a contract was received to start training courses consisting of forty short-service officers at a time, this to start in the following February. At the same time further VR contracts were signed with an increased number of 200 pilots, and, in addition, a fresh section was started for 200 aircrew (*ie non-pilots – Ed*). The increase in flying made it necessary to enlarge the airfield, and this was accomplished by removing the Nutfield sewage

---

[1]The author was slightly off the beam here. At the time of its formation, No 15 ERFTS was actually operating under the aegis of HQ Training Command, which had been established by redesignating HQ Inland Area on 1 May 1936. Reserve Command was not set up until 1 February 1939 and Flying Training Command did not enter the picture until as late as 27 May 1940 when Training Command was divided in two, the other half becoming Technical Training Command. **Ed**

farm, which had previously restricted the size of the landing area to 100 acres. Nobody was sorry to 'notice' its departure, and the area was further increased to 200 acres by taking in adjoining land.

Three complete direct entry courses were put through before the outbreak of hostilities in 1939, these being under the direction of Flt Lt J C Evans. Fg Off Adams had charge of the VR School, whilst the flying of the aircrew section was controlled by Fg Off G Mack. Unfortunately the six Avro Ansons with which they were to operate were held up for a time by lack of certain instruments, the first three only arriving in August 1939 very incompletely equipped.

Just before the war started, BAT Ltd, had organised No 56 Elementary and Reserve Flying School at Kenley Aerodrome, but this operated for only ten days before being closed down at the outbreak of hostilities. The equipment and personnel were transferred to No 15. Thus, at that date, there were twenty-nine Magisters, six Tiger Moths, nineteen Hart variants, four Battles and three Ansons at Redhill, the instructional strength having grown in proportion to twenty-nine. Two Link Trainers were in operation.

On the outbreak of war all training ceased and the aircraft were ferried away from Redhill, which was then, presumably, thought to be in immediate danger. The name of the unit was also changed to No 15 Elementary Flying Training School. In due course, the Magisters were returned to Redhill, but for the first few months of the war there was very little training done.

Between 11 September and 6 November certain qualified pupils were given instructors' courses, and Fg Off Douglas took over the post of CFI, Flt Lt Dale having left the unit. On 20 November, thirty-four qualified VR pilots were sent to the airfield for an eight-week refresher course which ultimately finished in March 1940.

On 1 January 1940, the flying personnel of the unit were completely mobilised, only the maintenance, ground school and accounts sections retaining their civilian status. Douglas became a squadron leader and commanding officer, combining with this the duties of CFI, whilst Flt Lt Macdonald came in as 'examining officer', this being before the days of a separate CFI on the establishment of EFTSs. On 1 March a testing and grading flight for Polish pilots was started under the aegis of Flt Lt J G ('Slim') Fletcher. This unit, entirely separate from No 15, had as its equipment Magisters and Fairey Battles.

With the advent of No 2 War Course on 28 March 1940, flying training at Redhill became organised on a wartime footing. True, we still managed to take tea on the lawn outside the mess and had most weekends 'off'; but with the invasion of the low countries matters were considerably speeded up and, in addition to their flying duties, both pupils and instructors found themselves having to take part in airfield defence preparations. It must, however, be admitted that it somehow fell to the lot of the pupils to do most of the trench digging.

Gone was the comparative peace of the Surrey air. Towards the middle of May we would occasionally hear great explosions coming from the south east, and constant streams of aircraft would go out in the morning and return in the evening. We would get into the habit of counting the number of aircraft of a squadron in the morning and again on their return; unhappily, the second evaluation was usually less than the first. On one evening we saw a number of Hurricanes coming in from the south-east, escorting sundry Bombays and Ensigns. Possibly, we then thought, the evacuation of Important Personages, but later we learned that it was probably a squadron returning from its erstwhile Continental base, complete with ground crews and spares.

Gone also, were our peaceful nights for, although we were not at that time disturbed by enemy raiders, there were multitudinous signals from 'Group', which usually arrived in the middle of the night marked 'Urgent' and which, when opened, were found to contain such things as promotions of NCOs. One night, however, an order to disperse all aircraft on the airfield arrived about midnight, to be put into operation at once. Only the CO, the Orderly Officer and the pupils were available, the instructors and others all being billeted widely around the neighbourhood; so those on the spot had to remove the forty-odd aircraft from the hangars, in pitch darkness, and taxi them to places round the perimeter of the landing area, all of which they did without mishap.

Came the 'Glorious First of June,' and the sight of the many trains, travelling almost guard's van to engine, on the main line which passed the aerodrome; they stretched for miles down the line and wherever they stopped the troops therein were greeted by everyone who was near. We flew over low and received waves from the carriage windows. (At least, we thought that the troops were waving, but we afterwards discovered that they may have been shaking their fists, as it was thought at the time that the RAF had let down the troops at Dunkirk.)

In the event of an invasion the humble Magister would have been committed to the fray. This one, No 15 EFTS's T9687, is fitted with bomb racks for just such an eventuality.

Later in the day things really began to happen. Some time previously, the CO had been told that he must hold himself in readiness to move the unit to a safer position should occasion arise, but he had always been given to understand that several weeks' notice would be given. Consequently it came as something of a shock when he was summoned to 'Command' to be told that No 15 EFTS was to evacuate itself in its entirety to Kingstown, Carlisle, and be working there in three days' time! Sunday, 2 June, was spent in frantic preparation, and during the day the Junior Course went off by coach, as did our baggage. Later, Lysanders of No 16 Sqn, which was to take our place at the aerodrome, began to arrive.

Fortunately, all but one of the school's aircraft were serviceable, so early on the morning of the 3rd these were made ready for the move to Carlisle, which was to be flown in two stages, with a stop at Shawbury to refuel. The armada took-off by flights, the organisation providing that one instructor, flying with a pupil, should lead some half-dozen other pupils, these latter flying solo. On the whole (and considering that none of the pupils flying had more than a few hours' solo to his credit) this went according to plan – except for the fact that when one of the C Flight instructors did the regulation circuit after take-off, the pupil following him did not, with the result that the instructor found himself at the rear of his charges.

At Kingstown, 'intensification' was the order of the day. The Powers-that-Were decided that, as well as having their courses shortened, the unfortunate pupils would have to take part in airfield defence work as well, with the result that certain of them were on duty day and night, with distressing results to the school's very moderate accident rate. This spate was not helped by the small size of Kingstown when compared with Redhill. However, things gradually stabilised and, between June 1940 and August 1941, seventeen complete elementary courses wcrc put through, these including both English and Polish personnel, the latter being supplementary to the advanced Polish Flight. In addition, satellite landing grounds were opened at Burnfoot and Kirkpatrick. At the latter site, night flying began in July 1941. Tiger Moths were used, as the Magisters were not then fitted for night flying. During the end of 1940 and in early 1941 the instructors were on duty from before dawn until after sunset, which was a great strain at the time. The civilian ground staffs worked even harder.

At Redhill, formation flying had been barred by those in authority, owing to the supposed risk of confusion with enemy aircraft; but after the school had settled down at Carlisle, B Flight's commander (Flt Lt D L Townsend) decided that if he reintroduced this exercise, even though only for instructors, and made it the first flight of the day, he might stand a better chance of getting everyone off the ground by 0830 hrs, which was the time flying duty commenced. Consequently the first ten minutes of each day was spent thus, the aircraft afterwards dispersing to their more lawful occupations. Nearby was Hadrian's Camp, one of our local defence points, and very early one morning (when the Flight Commander was on leave) we so far forgot ourselves as to do an echelon peel-off over this spot, afterwards disappearing at high speed before the gunners reached their armament. We just beat them to it. One instructor, however, cut his dive a little too fine and hit the parade ground with his left wheel, causing severe damage to the oleo leg. Its subsequent collapse on landing at Kingstown took a lot of explaining away.

Towards the end of 1940, Sqn Ldr Douglas was posted to 'operations' his place being taken by the senior Flight Commander, Flt Lt F S Homersham DCM MM, a veteran of the first world war who was promoted to squadron leader and shortly afterwards to wing commander, as were all EFTS COs at about that time. Sqn Ldr Geoffrey Walker came in as CFI. And on the day that Sqn Ldr Homersham took over, No 15 EFTS made history and our formation efforts came to a very sudden stop.

It was the morning of 26 October, and there had been a hard frost during the night. The Magisters had, as was customary by then, been dispersed around the perimeter during the night and had, therefore, a thick coating of hoar frost on the upper surfaces of the wings. We should, of course, have known better than to take off under these conditions, but whilst knowing that ice on wings was a bad thing we did not then realise that frost could be much worse. We soon found out.

The formation moved off as usual and, halfway across the airfield, I realised that my air speed was reading 65 mph and that the aircraft was still firmly on the ground. A few seconds more and I saw that I was not going to get airborne before the boundary was reached; so I throttled back and prepared for the bump, the brakes being useless on the slippery grass. To cut a long story short, I ran through a heap of stones by the fence, which removed both undercarriage legs, continued through the fence, and finally came to rest in the middle of the Glasgow Road. I did nothing worse than bump my head on the windscreen support. Having got out, I was able to survey the *debris* around me. I had been in No 3 position, and No 5 on my left had just managed to get airborne, but had gone through *both* road fences, finishing up in a heap in the next field. Our leader had stopped short of the fence, as he, too, had wiped off his undercarriage legs and had also run into a small tent, which had stopped him going further. No 2, on his right, had got up to some ten feet in a semi-stalled condition, and then hit a small hangar, leaving one wheel and a wing on the roof and landing in a heap on the far side. No 4 had managed to stagger across the road, where he hit the roof of a small cottage, depositing his engine through the roof on to a bed, and the aircraft into a chicken run by the side of the house. Most fortunately there was no fire anywhere, and none of the crews was badly hurt.

On the evening of the accident a member of the school heard an 'eye-witness' account of the affair. It appeared that the five aeroplanes were flying along on a beautiful morning, high up in the air, when a mist suddenly came up and 'they all toppled to the ground'! Of such stuff are witnesses made.

Whilst this was a time of intense work, work which I think we carried out to the best of our ability, there were, of course, lighter moments. I recall that the first necessity when we arrived at Carlisle was a suitable low-flying area and it was soon found that the banks of the Solway Firth were ideal. And not only the banks, for at low tide there was a wide

This and the next page – Oops! – Kingstown, 26 October 1940.

expanse of fine hard sand which sufficed as an airfield for at least two machines on the first day we were there. Later on I spied a sweet young thing sunbathing therein and 'shot her up' – only to find to my horror that it was Mrs Douglas, the CO's wife! He later said that he couldn't understand how she could have recognised me at 'a height of 100 feet…..'

We started *ab initio* flying with Polish pupils after we had settled down at Kingstown, most of whom had a poor command of the English language. When they were ordered to go up and perform, say, aerobatics,

we would severely enjoin them: 'Now, no low-flying; understand?' and 'Yes, I understand,' would come the reply. Nevertheless, half an hour or so later R1853 or N3780 would be reported somewhere at 50 feet! Subsequent interrogation would produce an admission, but qualified with: 'I not understand!'

A squadron stationed at Aldergrove in Ireland had a Magister in which the boys used to fly over to the mainland when coming on week-end leave. One day the AOC of 51 Group was inspecting No 15 when the Maggie arrived – flat out at 150 feet right across the middle of our airfield. The pilot's wife had come to meet him and had been allowed into the main gate. As he descended from the Magister she tripped lightly across towards it, but Gp Capt Noakes had not been amused and *he* got there first. She tripped back, not so lightly – and so did the pilot, after the group captain had finished with him.

During the winter of 1941 and spring of 1942 the Tiger became the only equipment of the unit, the Magisters being put into store or ferried elsewhere. The type of work altered also, *ab initio* training in full being abolished, and the 'grading' of pupils beginning. This meant that each individual was given about eight hours' instruction, on which his future as a Service pilot was judged; and if he went solo in this time, or showed that he would probably do so without much further instruction, a man would then be posted overseas to one of the Empire Air Training Scheme schools where he would complete his elementary flying training, afterwards passing on to one of the many Service Flying Training Schools in the vicinity. It was on this facet of training that the school expanded to its maximum size; by 1945 there were 108 aircraft on the strength, together with seventy-three flying instructors, and it was the proud boast of the engineering staff that they could usually maintain 95 per cent serviceability. At this time two flights, A and B, flew from Kingstown; two more, C and D, from Burnfoot; and the others, E and F from Kirkpatrick. Burnfoot latterly became a self-contained unit.

There were changes, too, on the personnel side. The CFI, Sqn Ldr Walker, went on to 'ops' and was replaced by Sqn Ldr 'Peanut' Morrish, who in turn gave over the reins to Sqn Ldr E P ('Splash') Lash, one of the original nine instructors at Redhill, and up to that time, commander of B Flight. Except for a short period at Reading in 1945, Lash remained CFI until the school closed down. Whilst he was at Reading, Sqn Ldr K C Baker took his place at Carlisle. Wg Cdr Homersham remained CO until

At least one of No 15 RFS's post-war Tigers was still wearing its warpaint as late as 1950.

his demobilisation early in 1947, when his place was taken by Wg Cdr T M Scott, AFC. Homersham and Lash, incidentally, were each awarded a well-deserved AFC whilst Douglas, on operations, gained the DFC.

In 1945 came the redundancy of certain aircrews, with the result that the school started giving pre-AFU courses to a number of these people, and such work went on in a gradually decreasing scale until the end of 1947 when, on 31 December, the school ended that particular phase of its existence, having flown some 270 000 hours and given instruction to over 12 000 pupils.

Before concluding, mention must be made of some of the civilian staff who kept the aircraft in the air. None will forget J P O'Hara, who was the senior ground engineer before and throughout most of the war period, nor his assistants, 'Bill' Lloyd, J V Brindley (the present chief engineer) and 'Ernie' Parker. Nor must we forget Messrs Harding, Murphy, Taylor and Nolan, who helped look after our creature comforts in the mess and elsewhere around the Station.

On the close-down, British Air Transport Ltd returned to Redhill where the Redhill Flying Club had been reopened; and on 1 April 1948, the school was reformed as No 15 Reserve Flying School under the then new Volunteer Reserve regulations. Initially, there were six Tiger Moths and the first three instructors were Wg Cdr Scott (CO), Sqn Ldr Lash (CFI) and Flt Lt 'Paddy' Bevan, who was also one of the wartime instructors at Carlisle. By 1949, the number of Tiger Moths had grown to twenty-four, whilst a little later six Anson XXI aircraft had joined the school, and later still these were joined by two Oxfords, which were used for Fighter Control Unit training. In 1951 the Tigers began to be replaced by Chipmunks; at first two flights were so equipped, but before the end of 1952 the school had lost its last Tiger Moth. From then onwards, the Chipmunks were used to give refresher courses to already-qualified pilots and the Ansons were used for Navigational and Signals refresher courses.

And now with the final disbanding of the seven remaining Reserve Flying Schools we come to the last chapter, and the work of over seventeen successful years comes to a close. It is, I think, work that in years to come will find its own niche in the annals of Royal Air Force history. Although this article has spoken only of No 15 RFS, many of the things that happened, and the work that was done, must have been reproduced at the other units of the 'civilian air force' which functioned during the two decades; and it is the hope of the writer that he will have stirred up pleasant memories in the minds of those who had the privilege and good luck to have been part of the pattern, as well as paying some small tribute to their great work.

Credit: All Magister photographs courtesy of C A Nepean Bishop via the A J Jackson Collection.

Note: While it has nothing to do with 'reserves', and embarrassing as it may have been, no account of the wartime life and times of No 15 EFTS should be allowed to omit the tale of the theft of one of its aeroplanes from Carlisle. The alleged incident occurred in November 1942 when two German pilots, who had escaped from a POW camp, found their way onto the airfield at Kingstown. Representing themselves as Dutchmen, they persuaded the groundcrew to fire up a Magister in which they then took off. Their bid for freedom came unstuck when they got lost, which obliged them to put down in a field in East Anglia. They were taken to Horsham St Faith where their story continued to hold up until their cover was blown by a somewhat belated signal notifying all stations that the air force was seeking to recover its lost property.

Interesting – but is the story true? It has appeared in print elsewhere but I can find no reference to it in the records of HQ Flying Training Command, No 51 Gp, No 15 EFTS or RAF Horsham St Faith. Was this because the facts were suppressed at the time, or is the story apocryphal. Can anyone shed any light? **Ed**

ROYAL AIR FORCE HISTORICAL SOCIETY

The Royal Air Force has been in existence for over 80 years; the study of its history is deepening, and continues to be the subject of published works of consequence. Fresh attention is being given to the strategic assumptions under which military air power was first created and which largely determined policy and operations in both World Wars, the inter-war period, and in the era of Cold War tension. Material dealing with post-war history is now becoming available under the 30-year rule. These studies are important to academic historians and to the present and future members of the RAF.

The RAF Historical Society was formed in 1986 to provide a focus for interest in the history of the RAF. It does so by providing a setting for lectures and seminars in which those interested in the history of the Service have the opportunity to meet those who participated in the evolution and implementation of policy. The Society believes that these events make an important contribution to the permanent record.

The Society normally holds three lectures or seminars a year in London, with occasional events in other parts of the country. Transcripts of lectures and seminars are published in the Journal of the RAF Historical Society, which is distributed free of charge to members. Individual membership is open to all with an interest in RAF history, whether or not they were in the Service. Although the Society has the approval of the Air Force Board, it is entirely self-financing.

Membership of the Society costs £15 per annum and further details may be obtained from the Membership Secretary, Dr Jack Dunham, Silverhill House, Coombe, Wotton-under-Edge, Gloucestershire. GLI2 7ND. (Tel 01453-843362)

THE TWO AIR FORCES AWARD

In 1996 the Royal Air Force Historical Society established, in collaboration with its American sister organisation, the Air Force Historical Foundation, the *Two Air Forces Award*, which was to be presented annually on each side of the Atlantic in recognition of outstanding academic work by a serving officer or airman. The RAF winners have been:

1997	Wing Commander M P Brzezicki MPhil MIL
1998	Wing Commander P J Daybell MBE MA BA
1999	Squadron Leader S P Harpum MSc BSc MILT
2000	Squadron Leader A W Riches MA
2001	Squadron Leader C H Goss MA
2002	Squadron Leader S I Richards BSc

THE AIR LEAGUE GOLD MEDAL

On 11 February 1998 the Air League presented the Royal Air Force Historical Society with a Gold Medal in recognition of the Society's achievements in recording aspects of the evolution of British air power and thus realising one of the aims of the League. The Executive Committee decided that the medal should be awarded periodically to a nominal holder (it actually resides at the Royal Air Force Club, where it is on display) who was to be an individual who had made a particularly significant contribution to the conduct of the Society's affairs. Holders to date have been:

Air Marshal Sir Frederick Sowrey KCB CBE AFC
Air Commodore H A Probert MBE MA

SECRETARY
Gp Capt K J Dearman
1 Park Close
Middleton Stoney
Oxon
OX25 4AS
Tel: 01869 343327

MEMBERSHIP SECRETARY
(who also deals with sales of publications)
Dr J Dunham
Silverhill House
Coombe
Wotton-under-Edge
Glos
GL12 7ND
Tel: 01453 843362

TREASURER
John Boyes TD CA
5 Queen's Close
Stansted
Essex
CM24 8EJ
Tel: 01279 814225

EDITOR and PUBLICATIONS MANAGER
Wg Cdr C G Jefford MBE BA
Walnuts
Lower Road
Postcombe
Thame
OX9 7DU
Tel: 01844 281449